THINGS EVERY ANIME FAN SHOULD KNOW

Discover the Fascinating Origins, Genres, Iconic Series, Fandom Culture, and So Much More!

KAITO SATO

ISBN: 978-1-962496-18-6

For questions, please reach out to Support@OakHarborPress.com

Please consider leaving a review!

Just visit: OakHarborPress.com/Reviews

FREE BONUS

GET OUR NEXT BOOK FOR FREE!

Scan or go to:

OakHarborPress.com/Free

TABLE OF CONTENTS

INTRODUCTION 1

CHAPTER ONE 3

WHAT IS ANIME? 4

ORIGINS OF ANIME 5

DIFFERENCES BETWEEN ANIME AND WESTERN ANIMATION 5

UNDERSTANDING ANIME GENRES 8

BREAKDOWN OF POPULAR GENRES 9

WHEN THERE ARE MULTIPLE SUBGENRES. 11

THE DIFFERENCE BETWEEN SUBBED AND DUBBED 13

MANGA VS. ANIME: THE CONNECTION 14

CHAPTER TWO: A BRIEF HISTORY OF ANIME 19

THE GLOBALIZATION OF ANIME 20

THE EVOLUTION OF ANIMATION TECHNOLOGY IN ANIME 23

CHAPTER THREE: MUST-WATCH ANIME SERIES AND MOVIES 27

CULT CLASSICS.. 28

STUDIO GHIBLI 31

NOTABLE FAN FAVORITES 33

CHAPTER FOUR: ANIME CULTURE &
COMMUNITY 39

THE WORLD OF COSPLAY.............................. 40

ANIME CONVENTIONS 43

ANIME FANDOM ONLINE................................. 45

FAN ART AND FAN FICTION........................... 47

THE INFLUENCE OF ANIME ON FASHION .. 50

CHAPTER FIVE: EXPLORING ANIME
SUBCULTURES 55

THE WORLD OF *ISEKAI* 56

MECHA ANIME 61

SLICE-OF-LIFE ANIME....................................... 64

SPORTS ANIME 68

PSYCHOLOGICAL AND THRILLER ANIME .. 70

CHAPTER SIX: THE MUSIC OF ANIME 73

THE IMPORTANCE OF OPENING AND ENDING THEMES 75

FAMOUS ANIME SOUNDTRACKS 77

THE ROLE OF VOICE ACTORS 79

MUSIC AND CONCERTS IN THE ANIME WORLD 83

CHAPTER SEVEN: ANIME MERCHANDISE AND COLLECTIBLES 85

THE WORLD OF ANIME FIGURES 87

MERCHANDISE 87

HOW TO WATCH ANIME 88

CHAPTER EIGHT: UNDERSTANDING ANIME THEMES AND STORYTELLING 93

COMMON THEMES IN ANIME 94

THE ROLE OF JAPANESE FOLKLORE IN ANIME 96

SYMBOLISM AND HIDDEN MEANINGS IN ANIME 100

CHAPTER NINE: EXPLORING THE FUTURE OF ANIME 103

THE RISE OF STREAMING PLATFORMS 104

THE ROLE OF VIRTUAL REALITY AND AUGMENTED REALITY 107

THE FUTURE OF CGI IN ANIME 108

CHAPTER TEN: BECOMING A DEDICATED ANIME FAN 115

STAYING UP TO DATE WITH NEW ANIME RELEASES 117

SUPPORTING THE ANIME INDUSTRY 120

ANIME COLLECTING TIPS FOR BEGINNERS 122

BUILDING ON YOUR ANIME KNOWLEDGE 126

LIFELONG FANDOM 130

CONCLUSION 133

INTRODUCTION

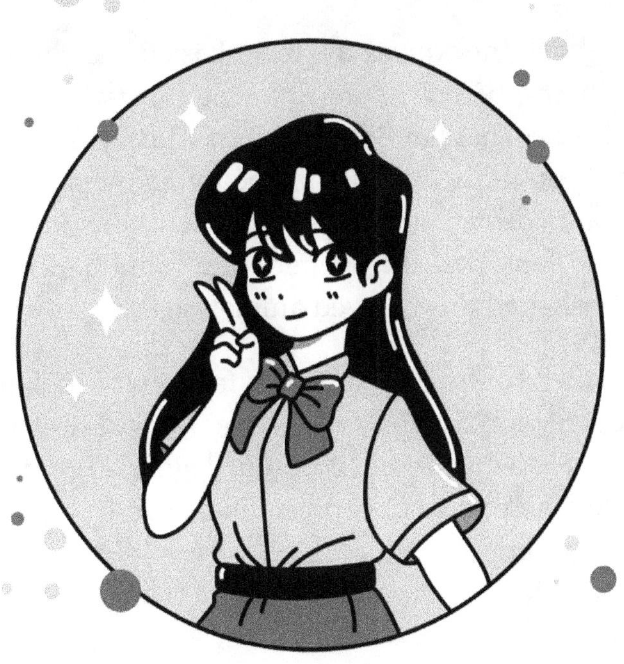

Prior to the 1990s, most people outside of Japan were unfamiliar with anime. Today, an estimated 600 million people consider themselves anime fans, with the demand for new content increasing by the day. From award-winning movies such as *Spirited Away* to famous franchises like Pokémon, anime has become a global touchstone for animation as a form of art and entertainment.

This book introduces the most basic concepts at the beginning before diving into the must-watch films and series that have shaped the industry. Along the way, you'll discover the impact of anime music, the vibrant cosplay and convention traditions that have united fans, and the deeper cultural influences that have shaped this beloved animation style.

Whether you're new to anime fandom or looking to deepen your existing knowledge, *Things Every Anime Fan Should Know* is your go-to guide to understanding and appreciating everything anime has to offer!

CHAPTER ONE

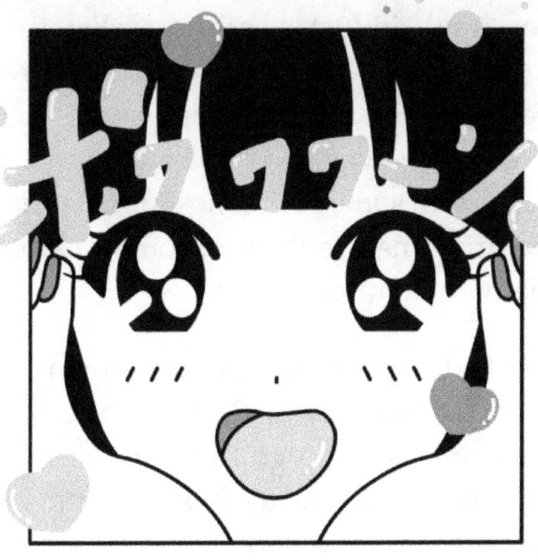

WHAT IS ANIME?

Anime is the Japanese word for "animation," and it includes all animation—no matter the place of origin. Outside of Japan, anime refers to a specific style of hand-drawn or computer-generated Japanese animation and industry creators. Before anime became a global sensation, cartoons were often associated with children's entertainment, especially in the West. However, Japanese anime caters to all age groups, with some of the most popular films and series featuring mature themes, complex story lines, and dynamic action sequences.

Often adapted from graphic novels known as *manga*, modern anime features distinct characteristics that give it an iconic and recognizable artistic style. This style is known for featuring block shading, vibrant backgrounds, and characters identified by their disproportionately large eyes.

With emotional story lines that focus on the human experience, anime appeals to diverse audiences. Genres include everything from romance to horror. For this and many other reasons, anime continues to grow in popularity around the world.

ORIGINS OF ANIME

In Japan, anime is defined as any type of animation, no matter where it's made. Outside of Japan, anime usually refers only to Japanese animation. There are examples of Japanese animation from as early as 1917. However, modern anime's roots really took hold and spread after World War II, especially with Osamu Tezuka's manga work, which impacted the artistic style and storytelling of anime. His influence in the early 1960s on *Astro Boy* was instrumental in expanding the anime industry and its appeal across the globe. The origins of anime are closely tied to Japanese culture, reflecting aspects of its history, religion, nature, folklore, and more.

DIFFERENCES BETWEEN ANIME AND WESTERN ANIMATION

The culture of anime has become internationally prolific and can be seen in movies, television series, memes, social media, fan fiction, and many other forms of entertainment that aren't strictly Japanese. Yet overall, there are still distinct differences between anime and Western animation in terms of aesthetics and storytelling.

For example, anime is often recognizable for its distinct artistic style. Characters often have exaggerated features such as eyes and hair, and backgrounds have detailed, fantastical landscapes with complex color palettes.

Anime is also known for its stylized kinetic action, conveyed through dynamic lines and other elements. Western animation, like productions from Disney and DreamWorks, typically features a less complex and detailed animation style in favor of more "realistic" backgrounds and characters with fluid movements.

In addition, anime differs in plot and narrative style. Whereas Western animation usually features a broad and straightforward plot based on linear action, anime tends to offer complicated stories centered on emotional themes and character development.

Western animation is also primarily focused on an individual protagonist and tends to follow a typical story arc of rising conflict, action, climax, and resolution. Stories often pair a "hero" with a "villain" in a simplified good-versus-evil narrative.

In anime, the focus is usually on a group of characters and their journey, with resolutions based on collectivism and collaboration. Anime themes tend to be broader than those of Western animation, ranging from social issues to philosophical ideas with characters that reflect complexities in human nature. Many Western animated works offer a "happy" ending in which "good" characters are rewarded and "bad" characters are either redeemed or face some sort of justice. Anime works are usually more thought provoking and ambiguous by not guaranteeing a simple happy ending.

In many ways, anime and Western animation also differ in their intended audiences. For decades, Western animation has been viewed primarily as entertainment for children. There are more exceptions now, as some Western animated works are expanding and geared specifically toward adult audiences. Anime, however, offers a more inclusive viewer approach, to some degree, by appealing to wider age ranges. Although genres such as *Kodomo* are intended for children, anime also features movies and series for teens and adults.

Despite their many differences between anime and Western animation, each has influenced the other in many positive ways. This has added to diversity in storytelling, creativity, and artistry in each industry.

UNDERSTANDING ANIME GENRES

Just like music, literature, cinema, and other art forms, anime has a variety of genres. Western audiences are often accustomed to seeing broad categories such as sci-fi, action, or comedy. However, anime is sorted into extremely specific categories. Some common examples include:

- *Isekai:* "Another world" stories where characters are transported to fantasy realms (e.g., *Sword Art Online, Re: Zero*).
- **Mecha:** Series with giant robots (e.g., *Gundam, Evangelion*)
- **Magical girl:** Young girls using magic to fight evil (e.g., *Sailor Moon, Madoka Magica*)
- **Slice-of-life:** Realistic character-driven stories (e.g., *Clannad, March Comes in Like a Lion*)

Anime often blends multiple genres seamlessly, whereas Western animation tends to follow a single dominant genre with minor elements. The most common Western blends are between two categories, such as science fiction and fantasy or mystery and thriller. In anime, though, it is common to see three or more genres masterfully mixed together. For example, *Attack on Titan* incorporates elements of action, horror, military, and political thrillers.

BREAKDOWN OF POPULAR GENRES

In addition to well-known, broad categories such as horror or romance, anime is further broken down into demographics based on the target audience. These include:

- ***Kodomo:*** For young children (e.g., *Doraemon, Pokémon*)
- ***Shōnen:*** For teen boys (e.g., *Dragon Ball, My Hero Academia*)
- ***Shōjo:*** For teen girls (*Sailor Moon, Fruits Basket*)
- ***Seinen:*** For adult men (e.g., *Berserk, Vinland Saga*)
- ***Josei:*** For adult women (e.g., *Nana, Paradise Kiss*)

Unlike other forms of animation, there are well over 30 main genres and countless subgenres in anime. The specificity of anime categories makes it easy for fans to discover new content that suits their interests. Although there are far too many genres and subgenres to cover in this chapter, the popular categories unique to anime include:

- **Cyberpunk:** Dystopian future and technology (e.g., *Psycho-Pass, Akira*)
- **Harem:** One protagonist surrounded by multiple love interests (e.g., *Tenchi Muyo!, The Quintessential Quintuplets*)
- ***Ecchi:*** Suggestive fan service (e.g., *High School DxD, To Love Ru*)
- ***Yaoi:*** Male/male romance (e.g., *Given, Junjou Romantica*)
- ***Yuri:*** Female/female romance (e.g., *Bloom Into You, Citrus*)
- ***Shounen-ai*** and ***Shoujo-ai:*** Lighter versions of boy love and girl love romances *(e.g., Yuri, Miss Kobayashi's Dragon Maid)*
- **Post-apocalyptic:** Survival after disaster (e.g., *Attack on Titan, Trigun*)
- **Idol:** Focus on pop idols (e.g., *Love Live!, The Idolmaster*)
- **Game:** Competitive gaming (e.g., *No Game No Life, Hikaru no Go*)
- **Sports:** Competitive team-based stories (e.g., *Haikyuu!!, Kuroko no Basket*)

If there's a specific type of story you enjoy, chances are there's an anime genre to match your tastes.

WHEN THERE ARE MULTIPLE SUBGENRES

Although most anime movies and series fit into multiple subgenres, there is usually one that overshadows the others. Where an anime fits in the subgenre spectrum depends on multiple factors, including the core story arc, how the show or film will be marketed, and the first impressions given by the visuals. Fan and critic opinions also play a role.

THE STORY ARC

Sometimes, deciding on a primary subgenre is easy based on the narrative's focus. For example, imagine an anime with both romance and mecha. Looking at the plot will help determine the main subgenre. If the plot is primarily focused on politics and piloting mechs, then the main subgenre is most likely going to be mecha. If the narrative is driven by a love triangle or romantic drama, then romance will be the main subgenre.

MARKETING AND DEMOGRAPHIC LABELING

As many anime story plots are complex and layered with multiple subgenres, it's sometimes easier for creators to use demographics and marketing goals when labeling the primary subgenre. This process involves looking at the age range and gender profile of the target audience. The complexity of the dialogue and themes is another major consideration. The *shōnen* subgenre is aimed at teenage boys, so most themes are easy to understand with simple language.

Other times, when there are multiple subgenres present, creators will choose whichever subgenre is the most popular for marketing reasons. *Isekai* anime is currently trending, so if there were many competing subgenres, this is the one that will most likely be used for sorting the work into categories on streaming platforms or search engines.

FIRST IMPRESSIONS AND VISUALS

Sometimes, the subgenre is based on the visual impression left by the anime's poster or pilot episode. If the promotional art has magical girls striking poses, it will probably fall under the magical girl subgenre. If there is blood or violence, the marketing team might label it as horror or action.

FAN AND CRITIC CONSENSUS

Public opinion often influences the primary subgenre over time as fans discuss the anime on forums or fan pages. For example, *Neon Genesis Evangelion* is clearly mecha, but because of fan feedback, it's often considered a psychological drama or existential thriller.

THE DIFFERENCE BETWEEN SUBBED AND DUBBED

Fans of anime who are not familiar with the Japanese language often have the options of "subbed" and "dubbed" formats. Subbed anime means that the original actors' voices are used in Japanese, but subtitles are available in the language preferred by the viewer.

When anime is dubbed, there are no subtitles. Instead, the narration and dialogue are voiced by actors in the language preferred by the viewer, rather than the original Japanese actors.

Some anime offers both subbed and dubbed versions, whereas others are only available as one type. Streaming services have helped make each format more accessible so that viewers have a greater number of options.

THE PROS AND CONS OF EACH

Viewers of anime may find that both subbed and dubbed formats have their pros and cons. Subbed anime preserves the quality and original form and allows viewers to hear the original Japanese language and acting.

Dubbed anime offers the convenience of not having to focus on subtitles. Viewers can instead direct their attention to the visual content. Another benefit is the improved accessibility for viewers with learning disabilities or reading challenges.

Ultimately, for non-Japanese speakers, the choice between subbed or dubbed anime depends on how each individual wants to view the material. Some fans may prioritize the authenticity of the original Japanese version, while others prefer to avoid the reading that comes along with subtitles.

MANGA VS. ANIME: THE CONNECTION

Manga is the term for Japanese graphic novels and comic books. Anime has a connection to manga in the same way animated cartoons have a connection to comic books. In other words, manga is like the "book" version of anime. These graphic novels feature similar illustration styles, themes, and storylines. In general, manga is often the source material for anime, but there are exceptions. Both forms play an important role in Japanese culture, and fans enjoy them in different ways.

When manga is adapted into anime, it's like bringing a static work from print to life with movement and color. However, there's an expectation that anime creators and producers will work closely with manga publishers to remain loyal to the original material, which is often highly regarded among fans.

HOW MANGA IS ADAPTED INTO ANIME

Manga is part of Japan's national culture, and its creation is attributed to Osamu Tezuka. Manga works can either be traditionally published or self-published.

The process of adapting manga into anime usually starts with the production company licensing the rights to the manga. The creators and producers must plan budgets, episode counts, and release schedules. Then they adapt the story into a script that will fit an animated movie or series and create storyboards to visualize each scene. Once cast, voice actors perform their recordings and animators produce the visuals. Music and sound effects are added later. The editing and post-production process ensures that the anime is ready for release.

Adapting manga into anime can present many challenges such as changing the pace of plotlines to fit the set number of episodes and fixing dialogue for audio flow. Occasionally, an anime series will catch up with the manga's storyline, leading to filler episodes and additional content that isn't part of the original print story.

The visual interpretation and animation style must also do justice to the original manga in terms of characters and background design. Technological advancements such as computer-generated imagery (CGI) have helped to streamline this process, but some viewers find this to be a compromise in visual quality.

Manga adaptations can also pose a financial risk to anime studios even if the manga work is already popular. An anime series episode costs $100,000 on average, meaning a full season may cost over a million dollars to make.

DIFFERENCES BETWEEN MANGA AND ANIME STORYTELLING

Manga and anime share similarities, but their content is produced and delivered in different ways. Manga books are often printed in black and white, making manga somewhat less expensive to produce and requiring fewer artists. Most manga works have the same author and illustrator, known as the *mangaka*. Meanwhile, anime is based on movement. It requires a production team of artists, musicians, and voice actors, among others.

In terms of storytelling, some people consider manga to be more original since its content is usually the sole creation of the *mangaka*. In contrast, many anime series and movies are based on stories that already exist.

Anime adaptations of source material that are already available, often in manga or light novel form, are more cost effective than creating a storyline that's completely original. In addition, anime that's adapted from existing stories is likely to already have a dedicated fan base.

CHAPTER TWO:
A BRIEF HISTORY
OF ANIME

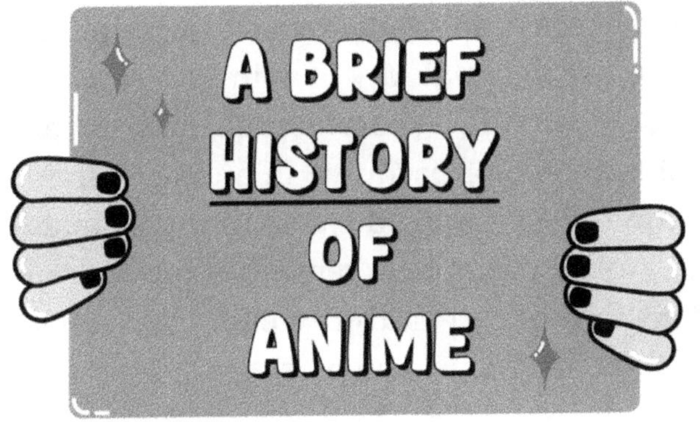

THE GLOBALIZATION OF ANIME

Not long ago, anime fans outside of Japan were considered a niche audience, and even the term *anime* itself would have been unfamiliar to many people. Today, anime is a global phenomenon that's very much part of mainstream entertainment among viewers from all backgrounds.

One of the most important factors that has influenced the huge rise in popularity of anime outside of Japan is the diversity of its storytelling. Viewers can find almost any type of narrative in anime genres, from the action of *shōnen* to the romance and fantasy of *shoujo*. Anime promotes a sense of connection among humans through art and storytelling that transcends geography, language, and more.

HOW ANIME BECAME POPULAR WORLDWIDE

Modern anime has been popular in Japan since the 1960s. In the 1980s and 1990s, anime spread to other countries as VHS tapes and DVDs created a marketplace outside of Japan. During that time, distribution of anime and manga content increased in the U.S.

However, the Pokémon franchise truly brought anime into the mainstream in the late 1990s. It grossed billions of dollars in anime, movies, and trading cards. By the 2000s, television shows such as *Pokémon, Yu-Gi-Oh!, Digimon, Sailor Moon,* and *Dragon Ball Z* were popular in the West.

Cartoon Network's Toonami featured many of these series, and related anime merchandise yielded huge sales. This resulted in large U.S. investments in Japan's anime industry and even more releases worldwide, including Hayao Miyazaki's Oscar-winning movie *Spirited Away* in 2001. Global audiences began to recognize and appreciate the unique animation quality and universal themes of anime.

In addition, many current celebrities, including Keanu Reeves and Megan Thee Stallion, have publicly expressed their love of anime in interviews or through social media posts. Celebrity endorsements inspire fans to give anime a try, making it an important part of pop culture.

More recently, the COVID-19 pandemic heavily influenced the worldwide popularity of anime. As people quarantined at home and relied heavily on streaming services for entertainment, millions of viewers discovered the appeal of anime. A strong fandom across social media also established a greater sense of connection and lessened feelings of isolation while people were in "lockdown." Many viewers used anime as a form of escape from the unusual stress and anxiety caused by the pandemic and have continued to find comfort in anime art and storytelling.

THE ROLE OF FANSUBS AND ONLINE STREAMING PLATFORMS

Fansubs and online streaming platforms have both contributed to the globalization of anime. An anime fansub is a movie or series that has been translated and subtitled into a different language by one or more fans. This is different from a sub anime, which is an official, licensed translation.

Although online fansub distribution is a form of anime piracy, fansubs have made many anime shows with a limited release accessible to international viewers. This has, in turn, heightened demand and increased official distribution deals.

Of course, the quality of translations and subtitles varies for fansubs, but they have undoubtedly made older and niche anime available to a wider audience. Therefore, even though it's technically an illegal practice, fansubbing has increased global demand for anime.

As access to online streaming platforms has grown across the globe, so has the exposure of anime movies and series. Services such as Crunchyroll, Netflix, Disney+, and Prime Video have made anime a mainstream staple for a wide and diverse audience. This growing popularity fuels the anime industry in creating new, unique content as well as supporting existing shows.

THE EVOLUTION OF ANIMATION TECHNOLOGY IN ANIME

The effect of technology on anime can cause intense debate among industry professionals and fans alike. Although there have been landmark advances in the evolution of animation technology, some find their implementation to be intrusive and even degrading to the art form as a whole. Critics believe that digital tools come at the expense of traditional human creativity.

Of course, animation technology offers immense benefits in terms of production time and costs. The use of CGI and advanced software allows for animated effects and visual creations that would be next to impossible for human animators to achieve unassisted. Digital animation also makes room for more anime content to be created at a much quicker pace, thereby increasing the number of options available for fans to enjoy and potentially reducing the time lag between seasons.

On the other hand, many anime fans are critical of the lack of human artistic value that comes from digital animation as it replaces hand-drawn traditions. Knowing that an anime movie or series contains the personal touch of human animators and artists can enhance the significance of the content.

FROM HAND-DRAWN TO DIGITAL ANIMATION

The roots of most anime begin with manga. Giving movement to flat illustrations through traditional hand-drawn animation retains the two-dimensional aesthetic and quality. Although digital animation techniques have been part of anime productions since the 1980s, many anime fans find computer-generated, three-dimensional renderings of characters and worlds to be too much of a departure from the hand-drawn visuals of classic anime.

In the early 1980s, computers were used to generate models and action sequences that were too difficult to achieve through traditional animation. These effects and CGI technology have made huge advancements, allowing for complex images and dynamic action in modern anime. For example, *The First Slam Dunk* and *Dragon Ball Super: Super Hero* are recent releases that have embraced 3-DCG anime. This style utilizes 3-D models and movement in combination with 2-D aesthetics such as flat planes and defined outlines. While some viewers feel this creates more of a video game look, 3-DCG anime is becoming more prevalent.

THE ROLE OF CGI IN MODERN ANIME

CGI plays an influential role in modern anime, from enhancing animated details to creating fully computer-generated anime works. In fact, recent 3-DCG productions have become high-grossing commercial successes despite wariness and outright complaints among some viewers. Certain CGI images and effects can appear hasty and poorly done. However, CGI is likely to remain impactful in its modern anime role, especially since it allows for a less expensive and easier production process.

Thankfully, there may be an occasional happy medium between the use of CGI and traditional animation techniques in modern anime. For example, Hayao Miyazaki, founder of Studio Ghibli, received great praise for the hand-drawn style of 2023's *The Boy and the Heron*, much of which was illustrated on paper with paint and pencil. Yet the movie also incorporates CGI elements for visual effects and digital compositing. These computer-animated details, however, are small and don't interfere with the classical anime style of the movie.

Essentially, anime works such as *The Boy and the Heron* demonstrate that 2-D, hand-drawn animation can be the core of animation with CGI complementing that style. However, this approach requires a team of trained animators, as well as additional production money, that isn't necessary with CGI.

CHAPTER THREE: MUST-WATCH ANIME SERIES AND MOVIES

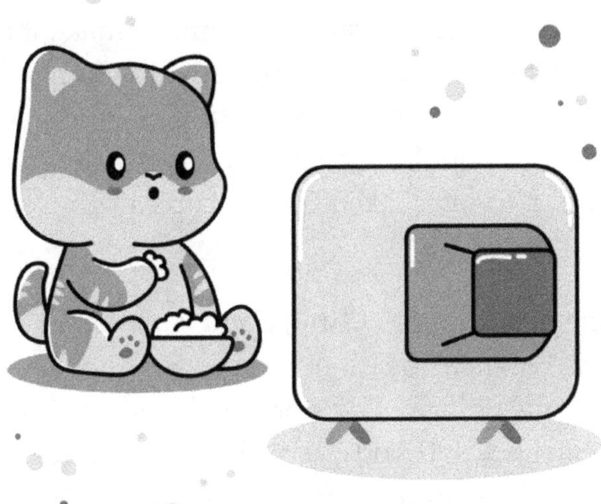

Anime fans are often quite loyal to certain series and movies. It would take an entirely separate book to go over every popular work. The list below is only a handful of some of the most iconic anime favorites.

CULT CLASSICS

GHOST IN THE SHELL (1995)

Ghost in the Shell was the first anime to make it to the top of the Billboard charts. Initially, the film seemed destined for failure following a box office flop. It didn't gain popularity until its home video release, which led to over 200,000 VHS copies being sold in the summer of 1996.

Directed by Mamoru Oshii, *Ghost in the Shell* is based on the manga by the same name created by Masamune Shirow. The story explores the boundary between soul and body as well as themes regarding what defines humanity. Its cyberpunk aesthetic, deep philosophical themes, and strong female lead changed public opinion about anime's limitations.

The story follows Major Motoko Kusanagi, an elite cyborg agent tasked with hunting a hacker known as the Puppet Master. Throughout her investigation, she starts to question the nature of her own existence, her memories, and what it means to be human.

Without revealing any major spoilers, Motoko eventually faces a revelation that blurs the boundaries between man, machine, and consciousness.

COWBOY BEBOP (1998–1999)

This genre-blending space Western follows a band of bounty hunters and their data dog, Ein, as they chase criminals across the galaxy aboard their space craft, the *Bebop*. Directed by Shinichirō Watanabe, the film's framing, pacing and visual composition redefined the limitations of TV anime.

Each episode was staged to mimic a self-contained film. The show blends elements of noir, spaghetti Western, Hong Kong action, and French New Wave cinema. Yoko Kanno delivers a revolutionary soundtrack featuring jazz, blues, funk, and rock influences. The unique style adds emotional depth and soul to the already iconic anime series.

AKIRA (1988)

Set in post-apocalyptic Neo-Tokyo, *Akira* is one of the most influential and visually stunning anime films ever made. This was one of the first films to present anime as serious adult storytelling and challenge Western stereotypes about cartoons. A pivotal film in the cyberpunk genre, *Akira* explores deep philosophical themes such as government corruption and existential dread.

The groundbreaking film pulled inspiration from the Bōsōzoku biker gangs that emerged in post-WWII Japan and follows the journey of a teen biker named Tetsuo Shima. Tetsuo Shima and his gang leader friend, Kaneda, are drawn into a government conspiracy involving secret labs, psychic children, and the legendary force known as Akira. This film went on to inspire the anime boom of the 1990s and 2000s. It also had a significant impact on the evolution of the cyberpunk anime genre as a whole.

PERFECT BLUE (1998)

This psychological horror/thriller dives deep into the fragmentation of identity and sanity. Directed by Satoshi Kon, the film destabilizes the viewer by shifting between layers of reality, dreams, performance, and hallucination. The meta-narrative style went on to influence countless films, including *Black Swan* and *Requiem for a Dream*.

TRIGUN (1998)

Trigun helped define the space Western subgenre with its reimagining of the American Wild West through a sci-fi lens. The protagonist, Vash the Stampede, is a pacifist on a desert planet brimming with saloons, bounty hunters, outlaws, and violence.

The action-comedy combines slapstick with tragic themes of war, loss, and trauma.

SAMURAI CHAMPLOO (2004)

Samurai Champloo made waves within anime communities for masterfully combining Edo-period samurai dramas with modern hip-hop culture. Elements such as the lo-fi soundtrack and graffiti aesthetics help marry traditional Japanese storytelling with current art forms. The story follows two samurai and a young woman tracing threads of clues regarding her father, who she only knows as the Sunflower Samurai.

STUDIO GHIBLI

In 1985, Hayao Miyazaki, Isao Takahata, and Toshio Suzuki founded Studio Ghibli, which is often referred to as "the Disney of Japan." Studio Ghibli has since become a household staple for many families internationally. Each film is known for its deep, poetic themes, striking aesthetics, and whimsical music scores.

Hayao Miyazaki is regularly referred to as "the greatest living animator." His films often involve strong female leads, anti-war themes, flying machines, nature worship, and ambiguous morality.

Some people outside of Japan may find aspects of Studio Ghibli films confusing, as many of the stories are based on traditional Japanese folklore. Despite retiring multiple times, Miyazaki keeps coming back with new films. His most recent production is *The Boy and the Heron*, which released in 2023.

SPIRITED AWAY (2001)

Spirited Away won an Oscar for Best Animated Feature. It's a magical coming-of-age story infused with Japanese folklore. The name itself is a reference to the Japanese belief of *kamikakushi,* or "hidden by kami," and refers to the sudden disappearance or death of a person.

PRINCESS MONONOKE (1997)

Princess Mononoke explores the relationship between humanity and nature. Its powerful message emphasizes interconnectedness and the consequences of unchecked industrialization.

MY NEIGHBOR TOTORO (1988)

My Neighbor Totoro is a wholesome comfort film that produced Studio Ghibli's mascot: Totoro. The story follows sisters Satsuki and Mei, who move to the countryside with their father after their mother is hospitalized for an undisclosed illness. The story emphasizes the healing power of nature and family.

HOWL'S MOVING CASTLE (2004)

Howl's Moving Castle (2004) is a love story wrapped in anti-war themes, magic, and steampunk vibes. In many ways, it's a classic "beauty and the beast" trope revisited through a Japanese lens.

GRAVE OF THE FIREFLIES (1988)

Grave of the Fireflies became known for being one of the most heartbreaking war films ever animated. This award-winning masterpiece follows a teenager named Seita, who is caring for his younger sister. The two children are separated from their parents after an American firebombing during World War II and must rely on each other to survive.

NOTABLE FAN FAVORITES

NEON GENESIS EVANGELION

On the surface, *Neon Genesis Evangelion* is a series about teenagers piloting giant robots to fight creatures called Angels. This mecha anime explores themes of depression, trauma, identity, and what it means to be human.

NANA

This film is a stylish, emotional drama about two young women named Nana who become roommates in Tokyo. One is a punk-rock singer chasing her musical dreams; the other is a hopeless romantic searching for love and purpose. This coming-of-age story falls under the slice-of-life genre.

FULLMETAL ALCHEMIST

In this series, Edward and Alphonse Elric suffer a tragic accident while trying to bring their mother back from the dead using alchemy, which leaves them with horrific physical scars. Set in a world where magic and science blend, the brothers' hope to find the philosopher's stone to restore their physical bodies. The series features themes of sacrifice, justice, war, and the consequences of playing God.

DRAGON BALL Z

This anime series is one of the most popular sagas and helped define the genre. An alien warrior named Goku trains and fights to protect Earth from increasingly powerful enemies. With explosive battles and iconic villains like Frieza, *Dragon Ball Z* is all about perseverance, friendship, and pushing past your limits.

MAWARU PENGUINDRUM

This surreal and emotional anime blends magical realism, mystery, and family drama. When their younger sister falls ill, two brothers make a deal with a mysterious spirit who lives inside a penguin-shaped hat. Beneath its quirky visuals lies a deep, symbolic story about fate, trauma, love, and the ripple effects of tragedy.

SAILOR MOON

This classic anime falls into the magical girl genre. Usagi Tsukino is a clumsy and kind-hearted teen who discovers she's a Sailor Moon, a guardian destined to protect the world from evil. Alongside her team, she fights monsters, falls in love, and learns what it means to be a hero.

POKÉMON

In this series, Ash Ketchum is a 10-year-old boy who dreams of becoming a Pokémon master. Following his birthday, he embarks on a quest that starts with obtaining his first Pokémon, Pikachu, and leads to a wild adventure involving Pokémon battles and thwarting the plots of villains like Team Rocket. This anime gained ground as a childhood favorite for many 1990s kids and has since become a household name. The franchise branched out from television to games and collectibles.

NARUTO

This film is about Naruto Uzumaki, an orphan with a mysterious fox spirit sealed inside him. Shunned by his village, he dreams of earning their respect by becoming the strongest ninja—the *Hokage*. This extremely popular anime is teeming with intense battles, emotional story arcs, and themes of perseverance.

ATTACK ON TITAN

Although technically considered a *shōnen* anime for teenage boys, *Attack on Titan* is a dark action-thriller featuring violent scenes and mature themes. The story follows Eren Yeager and his friends as they join the military to fight back against giant man-eating monsters called Titans.

ONE PIECE

This series centers on Monkey D. Luffy, a swashbuckling pirate seeking the legendary treasure known as the One Piece. This adventure follows him and his lovable crew as they sail to bizarre islands and encounter strange creatures and mysteries. The saga incorporates themes of freedom, friendship, and chasing your dreams.

INUYASHA

In this anime, Kagome Higurashi is a high school student who's transported back in time. She meets Inuyasha, a half-demon with a sharp temper and a tragic past. Together, they embark on a quest to find the shards of the Shikon Jewel, which grant immense power.

MOBILE SUIT GUNDAM

Mobile Suit Gundam blends intense robot battles with deep political drama as it explores the human cost of war and the ethical complexities of conflict. This series has spawned multiple spin-off series, movies, and alternative timelines, including:

- Gundam ZZ (1986)
- G Gundam (1994)
- Gundam Wing (1995)
- Gundam SEED (2002)
- Gundam 00 (2007)
- Iron-Blooded Orphans (2015)

CHAPTER FOUR: ANIME CULTURE & COMMUNITY

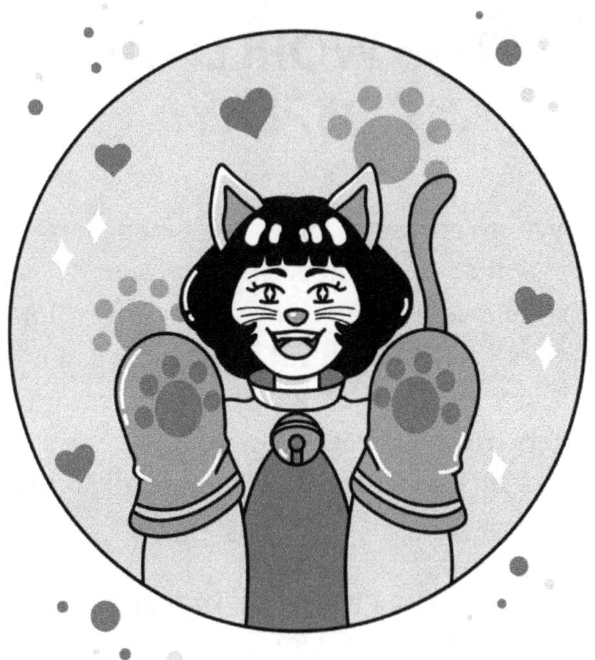

The level of camaraderie among creators and viewers is one reason that anime is such a special form of entertainment. Fans have developed in-person and online groups dedicated to anime works. There are also industry conventions so that fellow enthusiasts can gather, meet anime artists and voice actors, and express themselves through fan art. This community has fostered inclusivity in distinct ways, which has won it many lifelong fans.

THE WORLD OF COSPLAY

Cosplay, or costume play, is when fans wear costumes and accessories to represent a certain character. In many ways, cosplay is a form of role-playing and performance art where fans can interact with others as part of a subculture community. Characters from anime, manga, TV series, video games, comic books, and cartoons are all sources for cosplay.

Some people outside the world of cosplay may find it to be an odd hobby. However, researchers have found that cosplay offers benefits to participants' well-being, such as stress relief, social connection, and building confidence. Embodying a beloved character through building a particular look and costume can bring a sense of accomplishment. In addition, cosplayers have opportunities to interact with others who have similar interests. This can lead to new friendships and feelings of belonging and support.

THE RISE OF COSPLAY CULTURE

Cosplay is rooted in sci-fi fandom and conventions. In 1939, Myrtle Rebecca Douglas, better known as "Morojo," became the first-known costumer dedicated to cosplay. Morojo designed futuristic costumes that appeared at the first World Science Fiction Convention in New York City.

Cosplay culture grew out of this trend, but the Japanese word *cosplay* wasn't used until 1984 when Nobuyuki Takahashi wrote an article in the Japanese magazine, *My Anime*. Takahashi coined the word to describe costumed attendees instead of using the term *masquerade*, which had upper-class connotations.

However, cosplay isn't just about wearing a costume or trying to look like a specific character. It's also about *becoming* a character by mimicking their expressions, gestures, and patterns of speech. Cosplay culture has rapidly grown in Japan and many other countries, especially since the 1990s.

Most fan conventions feature cosplay events, and it's an integral part of anime fandom.

HOW TO GET STARTED WITH COSPLAY

To get started with cosplay, it's helpful to know and understand some basic tips. Many people start by cosplaying online and sharing personal videos. There may even be a local in-person group you can join. It may require some trial and error, but it's worth it to find the right medium and community for you.

Choose a character you connect with and love. It's also a great idea to research each character and find images, fan art, and other cosplayer photos for reference. Although some cosplayers value accuracy, you should work with what makes you feel comfortable and empowered.

Many cosplayers find inspiration and tips by interacting with fellow fans or even watching online tutorials. Cosplay videos often cover makeup, costumes, props, and acting skills. Some cosplayers purchase complete or partial costume sets and props, while others prefer their own handiwork. It's okay to start small and build the hobby from there.

Your costume doesn't have to be perfect. Like any hobby or activity, cosplay is about learning, self-expression, and connecting with others. Finding a positive and fun community should be your first priority, in addition to embracing the personal joy and creativity of cosplay.

ANIME CONVENTIONS

Anime fans attend conventions as a way to celebrate their interests, meet others, and learn more about Japanese animation and culture. Thousands of attendees gather each year at both large and small conventions around the world to share their love of anime.

Anime conventions typically feature events such as interviews and the chance to get autographs or buy special merchandise. Shared experiences such as these keep creators and fans engaged while celebrating anime as an important form of entertainment and pop culture.

Anime Expo and Comic-Con are two of the most well-known and popular conventions. Anime Expo is considered the largest North American anime and manga convention, attracting over 100,000 guests annually. It premiered in July 1992 in San Jose, California, before later relocating to southern California.

Meanwhile, Comic-Con began in San Diego in 1970 with a group of fans who shared a love for comics, movies, and science fiction. Since then, it has grown into a global institution and the world's most prominent arts convention.

One imperative for all convention attendees is to respect fellow fans and the overall community. Most conventions expect participants to follow policies and rules to ensure the experience is safe and positive for everyone. This includes adhering to policies about behavior and recording.

HOW CONVENTIONS BRING FANS TOGETHER

Anime conventions allow fans to engage at a variety of levels, depending on their interests and what they're comfortable with. Some attendees prefer to participate in cosplay, whereas others may decide to take on more of an observational role. Vendors also play a large role in bringing fans together at conventions by offering unique merchandise to support the industry.

There are also digital platforms that act as extensions of the physical space and experience. Several social media groups, forums, and even apps are designed for participants to keep in touch. This provides a sense of community beyond the convention events and benefits fans by facilitating networking opportunities.

ANIME FANDOM ONLINE

Anime has generated one of the largest networks of active online communities in internet history. This diverse global fandom, made up of millions, allows people to share ideas and learn new aspects of anime.

The online anime fandom features platforms such as dedicated websites, forums, subreddits, and social media pages. These formats have an international reach and generate discussions and engage different viewpoints from around the world.

HOW ONLINE COMMUNITIES FOSTER FANDOM

Online communities aren't bound by time zones or the need to coordinate schedules. You may find people on different continents who enjoy and appreciate the same anime. This creates opportunities for cultural exchanges, forming meaningful relationships, and developing a greater sense of community.

Unfortunately, not all online communities within the anime fandom will lead to positive experiences or productive interactions. Therefore, it's important to be selective regarding which platforms you join. Although it may be tempting to limit your interactions to online sites that echo your views, it's also wise to expand your interests by trying new shows and keeping an open mind.

EXPLORING FORUMS, SOCIAL MEDIA GROUPS, AND FAN SITES

There are forums, social media groups, and fan sites for nearly every level of anime fandom. To find what appeals to you, search online for a page dedicated to your favorite show or character. Certain streaming platforms also have forums where you can actively participate.

The best and safest way to navigate such online communities is to limit yourself to joining well-established sites. Participating in more obscure groups carries a much bigger risk of exposure to inappropriate content and harmful behavior.

Thankfully, most well-known and popular anime forums are safe, especially those with moderation teams to manage all content. You can also check for any legal concerns by ensuring that the platform abides by copyright laws and avoids illegal or pirated anime. Another sign of site safety is visible community guidelines to maintain respectful interactions among members and contributors.

While you're interacting with other fans, avoid engaging in any behavior that could be considered inappropriate and treat others with the same level of respect that you expect to receive in return.

If you are aware of any inappropriate content or phishing scams, report it to the moderator(s) of the site as soon as possible. Don't engage until the situation is resolved, and avoid sharing any identifiable data such as your phone number, address, passwords, financial information, etc.

FAN ART AND FAN FICTION

One unique and rewarding aspect of anime culture is the active participation of fans. Many anime enthusiasts create and share their own anime fan art and fiction—sometimes for small social circles and sometimes at a level that's visible across online communities. Fan creativity is an expression of love for the art form and part of the collective culture of anime.

THE ROLE OF FAN CREATIVITY IN ANIME

Fan creativity plays an important role in anime. Unlike many traditional forms of entertainment, anime allows for unique artistic contributions by fans. Many anime enthusiasts create fan art such as drawings or paintings of characters or favorite scenes.

Fan fiction is also common, featuring additional storylines from fans. Although fan fiction retains basic elements of the anime's story and characters, they aren't officially endorsed by the creators of the original material. Instead, these creative endeavors are a means of engagement by fans with the anime they love.

Since fan art and fiction aren't meant for commercial sale, it can benefit anime fandoms by providing members with an artistic outlet. For example, a fan may post a drawing of anime characters wearing different clothing or depict a scene through a different artistic interpretation. Other fans may write alternate character endings, backstories, or even additional plotlines.

PLATFORMS FOR SHARING FAN ART AND STORIES

There are many online anime communities where fans can post their creative work, including fan forums and subreddits. Social media platforms such as Pixiv, ArtStation, and DeviantArt also allow fans to create and share their portfolios while interacting with fellow artists.

Consider joining online communities that offer art or fiction contests as a means of presenting your creative work and receiving feedback. Many fans begin by posting their art and fiction on their own social media profiles. Platforms such as Facebook, X, and Instagram can be used to reach a wide audience, especially with the use of anime hashtags.

Another way to demonstrate your talent for fan art and fiction is to build a personal website. This allows you to show your growing portfolio and add context using descriptions and biographical details.

The most important thing to remember before sharing any fan art or fiction is to give credit to the original source, including the movie or series title and the names of any characters. Pay attention to copyright and only use work that is considered "fair use." This means that any reproduction of an anime character or story must be significantly modified so that it's not a direct copy of the original material.

Fan art and fiction that is fair use demonstrates that the artist/writer has created unique elements based on their own interpretations. Fans should also check platform policies and terms of service before sharing any content. Don't allow your creations to be used for any commercial reasons without specific, legal permission from copyright holders.

THE INFLUENCE OF ANIME ON FASHION

Anime has grown beyond a form of entertainment, impacting many aspects of culture and various industries—including fashion. Whether it's T-shirts featuring beloved characters or higher-end jewelry inspired by anime, fashion continues to embrace the creativity of anime.

Some fans have even created their own fashion styles that are inspired by anime aesthetics and designed to reflect their unique relationships with anime content. In fact, fashion is yet another conduit for anime lovers of all types to come together, share their passions, and create memories together.

Accessories and jewelry are also elements of fashion that have been influenced by anime. These range from bags and backpacks to necklaces and earrings, often with high-end prices. These accessories provide fashionable, detailed pieces for anime lovers and the opportunity for fans to embellish their personal styles.

HARAJUKU STYLE

Harajuku is a neighborhood in the commercial district of Tokyo. Harajuku fashion has a wide variety of styles subcultures that began with the proliferation of Japanese youth culture in the 1970s.

Since then, the Harajuku area has been associated with J-fashion stores and magazines. Harajuku fashion is known for being colorful and decorative, but there are some subgenres that include darker styles. It's also incorporated influential Western styles and alternative looks such as Lolita and Decora.

Anime has helped shape Harajuku fashion, mixing styles and subculture trends such that each person can independently craft their personal image. This appeals to young anime fans who recognize the importance of exploration and the rejection of rigid societal standards.

STREET WEAR AND ATHLEISURE

Anime has also had a significant influence on the growth of street-wear styles and new clothing lines that incorporate anime graphics. Anime characters and images often appear on everyday apparel, including hoodies, T-shirts, and sneakers. This impact on street wear appeals to a growing market of anime lovers and reflects a culture of self-expression.

In addition to street wear, graphic tees that represent specific anime characters, series, and movies have become an iconic fashion element. Anime is also an influence in sportswear, or "athleisure," fashion, including leggings, tracksuits, and even sports bras that feature anime graphics and design. Another benefit of anime's impact on street wear, sports, and lounge apparel is that fans have options for gender-neutral clothing that still incorporate favorite anime styles.

KAWAII FASHION

As the influence of anime grows in the world of fashion, so do anime-inspired iconic fashion elements. For example, *Kawaii* aesthetic culture has become even more iconic due to anime characters.

Kawaii fashion is colorful and cute, often with frills and childlike styles, some of which resemble anime characters.

CHAPTER FIVE: EXPLORING ANIME SUBCULTURES

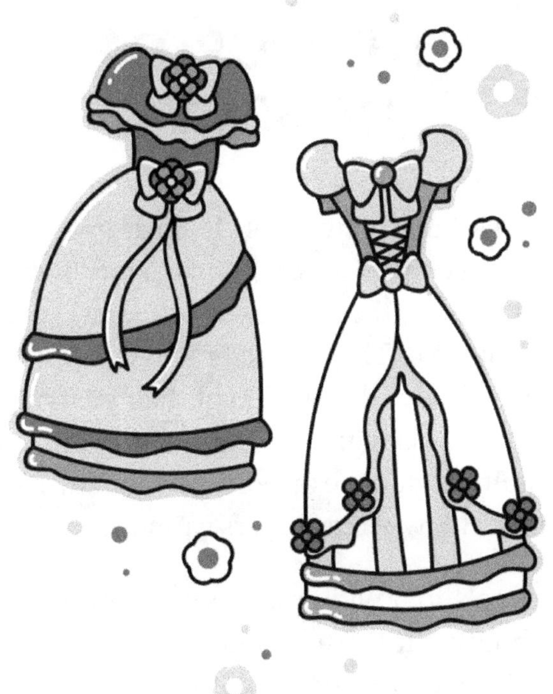

Like many art forms, anime features subcultures that appeal to different audiences and allow creators to explore diverse material, characters, and themes. However, it's important to note that labeling an anime movie or series as a particular subculture doesn't place limits on its scope. In other words, these subcultures represent a general sense of what viewers can expect of the plot rather than strict guidelines for the material.

THE WORLD OF *ISEKAI*

Isekai means "alternative world." In anime, it reflects a popular subculture encompassing storylines where a character finds themselves in a fantasy world or parallel universe. The character's new life is often a fresh start without the burden of their past mistakes, circumstances, or regrets. Some anime characters in this subculture gain the opportunity to return to their original world, whereas others cannot return.

Isekai appeals to a wide range of viewers, including those who may feel frustrated with or devalued by society. It offers a virtual escape from ordinary life through its hero protagonist as they navigate a new world.

The concept originated in Japanese folktales, like the ancient story of the fisherman Urashima, who saved a turtle and was transported to a kingdom under the sea. He then found himself returned to his village centuries in the future. *Isekai* also took modern root in novels such as *Warrior from Another World* and series such as *Aura Battler Dunbine*.

The two primary types of *isekai* are transition and reincarnation. In transition *isekai*, the main character is transported to another world by travel or a magical summons. In reincarnation *isekai*, the main character dies in their "real" world and is "born" into another.

Interestingly, the 1986 anime film adaptation of the video game *Super Mario Bros.*, in which Mario plays a video game that comes to life, is considered an early *isekai* version of a protagonist who's trapped in a video game. The 1990s saw many anime series with *isekai* tropes, and the 2001 movie *Spirited Away* is one of the first *isekai* anime to be seen worldwide.

UNDERSTANDING *ISEKAI* TROPES

Some main characters in *isekai* series are ordinary individuals who must learn new skills and magic when transported to their new life. An ordinary character is often seen as extraordinary in the second world, especially if the world they're sent to is less advanced than the modern "real" world.

Other series feature a hero who already possesses some sort of special ability before they experience *isekai*. For example, the hero may be transported into a video game world when they already know how the game works. This meta knowledge typically allows the hero to be crafty and avoid a bad ending. To balance this, a series may include outside factors or characters to disrupt the story so that the hero must adjust their reliance on meta knowledge.

There are many other tropes in the *isekai* subculture. A common convention is the main character pursuing a goal in the new world. Other tropes include joining a guild, which allows the main character to have a sense of belonging and creates a team of secondary characters to support the hero's journey. This trope is closely related to another *isekai* convention where the protagonist is overpowered and must learn to fight alongside their new comrades.

THE APPEAL OF *ISEKAI* SERIES

Isekai series have captivated audiences since the early 2010s, and they are prevalent on streaming platforms such as Netflix and Crunchyroll. Much of their appeal is rooted in escapism and living a fulfilling life vicariously through *isekai* characters. *Isekai* heroines are especially popular among female anime fans for their ability to live in the manner they choose without gender limitations.

Digimon was one of the first *isekai* anime series. The Digimon franchise offers an anthology of new stories for each series. However, there's an *isekai* foundation to the basic plot, which usually involves a group of kids who pair with powerful Digimon creatures and travel to the Digital World to save the Digimons' home.

Here are other examples of top *isekai* anime works and what makes them unique:

- ***I'm in Love with the Villainess***: Rei Ohashi is reincarnated into Rae Taylor, the protagonist of the game Revolution. This series is unique in that Rae is openly gay and pursues a relationship with the villainess Claire Francois. *I'm in Love with the Villainess* incorporates LGBTQ+ content through a thoughtful and meaningful version of *isekai*.
- ***Ascendance of a Bookworm***: In this series, protagonist Urano Motosu is dying in the real world but wishes to be reborn because of her love of reading. Urano is reborn into a new world as a kid named Myne, but it's before the invention of the printing press, making books a rarity. This *isekai* is

unusual in that the main character is not a warrior hero. Instead, Myne decides to spread her love of literature in the new world with the goal of hand-copying books she's read from memory.

- ***That Time I Got Reincarnated as a Slime:*** This fantasy *isekai* series finds Rimuru Tempest reborn in a new world as a slime with magic powers. Rimuru becomes friends with his fellow characters due to his charm, which makes the series lighthearted and fun for viewers.

- ***The Boy and the Heron:*** This *isekai* film follows young Mahito Maki, who has lost his mother in the Pacific War. He meets a talking heron in his mother's former home. The heron transports Mahito to another world and promises that he can bring Mahito's mother back. *The Boy and the Heron* is a beautiful and emotional anime movie about overcoming loss.

Ultimately, fans of this anime subculture appreciate the potential for escape and learning about a new world along with the protagonist. Many find the characters and their alternate worlds to be therapeutic, especially in embracing the idea of a fresh start in a new place.

MECHA ANIME

Mecha is an anime subculture that involves mechanical creations and robots in battles. Mecha series often incorporate drama, comedy, and a great deal of action. Science fiction is influential in mecha anime subculture, but series differ in whether the robots are created through science or magical means.

Although the mecha anime genre doesn't exclusively feature robots, there are two types of robots that are likely to be part of mecha series. Giant or super robots tend to be singular creations with mythical powers derived from scientists or ancient civilizations. Certain robots may also be combined with others to form even greater and more powerful robots. The other type of robot often featured in mecha anime is known as "real." These robots are based in science and are usually mass produced for battle or war.

The mecha anime subculture is rooted in the period after the end of World War II. Japan experienced growth in its economy and technology, leading to two series that are considered the foundations of mecha. *Astro Boy* depicts the adventures of an android with human emotions, while *Gigantor* centers around a young boy who inherits a giant robot from his scientist father.

These series gained fan bases in Japan and beyond, popularizing story lines in which robots would battle other robots or monsters. Mecha anime reached its peak in Japan in the 1970s and 1980s, but the genre still continues today in contemporary anime.

A CLOSER LOOK AT GUNDAM AND EVANGELION

Initially, mecha anime series were based on monster-of-the-week storylines. Typically, a giant robot would face a different robot or monster and triumph in battle. Then the scenario would be repeated during the following episode or volume.

However, in 1979, *Mobile Suit Gundam* changed this pattern within the mecha genre by devising a space saga featuring genocide, intergalactic war, and epic battles among gundams, or giant robots. Gundam has been adapted many times as a military science fiction anime series, becoming a franchise and making a big impact on Japanese culture and mecha subculture.

Yoshiyuki Tomino developed *Mobile Suit Gundam*, which was originally titled *Freedom Fighter Gunboy*. The series was designed for a teenage male audience, featuring high-capability Gundams that are bipedal, humanoid vehicles controlled by human pilots.

Gundam pilots are typically Newtypes, a group of advanced humans with psychic abilities. They use specialized mobile suits and can sense one another through space. *Mobile Suit Gundam* is credited with establishing the "real robot" subgenre of mecha anime subculture through its technology and realistic weapons design that reflect limitations and even malfunctions.

Hideaki Anno's 1995 *Neon Genesis Evangelion* was an innovative series that changed the mecha genre by incorporating a darker and more mystical story. The emotional and behavioral traits of the characters suggest Freudian and Jungian psychoanalytic influences in addition to other philosophical elements present in the story, which is set in the futuristic city of Tokyo-3.

Shinji Ikari, the main character, is a teen boy who joins the group Nerv as his father's recruit. Nerv is an organization of pilots who battle Angels with Evangelion—a giant biomechanical mecha. The series is considered among the best anime as it explores human emotions and experiences. It has also served as the basis for several films with different plots and endings.

THE IMPACT OF MECHA ON SCI-FI AND ANIME CULTURE

There has been a reciprocal impact between mecha, sci-fi, and anime culture. Over the decades, the outlook and tone of mecha anime has changed.

For example, in the 1950s, there was a sense of hope and earnestness related to advancements in science, whereas the mood of 1990s mecha anime was much darker with cyberpunk and dystopian themes. This shift is likely due to the growing awareness among humans of the potential to misuse science and technology for destructive purposes—a recurring theme in science fiction overall.

Mecha anime utilizes robot concepts, intense character development, and action to explore complex societal issues such as ethics and humanity. Mecha protagonists symbolize the relationship between humans and technology, in addition to the psychological pressures of war.

SLICE-OF-LIFE ANIME

Slice-of-life is another anime subculture that's widely popular and resonates with audiences. This type of anime series is focused on simple, everyday moments and relatable characters who become special or memorable.

Since slice-of-life anime portrays realistic life events rather than magical adventures or dramatic action, it tends to have a slower pace. These stories center around character interactions, problem-solving, feelings, and individual growth. They also feature recognizable settings such as school, home, and work environments in which viewers can imagine themselves.

WHAT MAKES SLICE-OF-LIFE ANIME UNIQUE

Slice-of-life series gained popularity in the mid-1980s. They are unique in the world of anime due to their focus on relatable experiences rather than alternative worlds or intense conflict. This allows creators to access a vast range of narrative possibilities based on realism.

Storylines such as challenges with friends or romance allow viewers to form emotional ties to characters' lives. In addition, slice-of-life anime presents a range of subtle themes that can be lighthearted or more serious and impactful. Characters tend to have warm interactions and positive arcs, which many viewers find to be comforting.

CLANNAD

Clannad (2007–2009) is unique among slice-of-life anime. It begins as a typical series where the main characters fall in love and resolve their issues. However, there is a continuation of their journey in *Clannad After Story*. This goes beyond the slice-of-life formula of the first series, which already has an established audience who knows that the characters have achieved their initial goals.

Clannad's structural change and emotional shift in the second series allows the audience to see what happens after the "happy ending." Tragedy occurs, and the main character must face harsh realities made up of sorrow and emotional pain. Although there are magical elements within the plot, *Clannad*'s series puts a new spin on the typical slice-of-life story.

MARCH COMES IN LIKE A LION

March Comes in Like a Lion (2016–2018) is another popular slice-of-life anime series. It centers around an introverted character named Rei Kiriyama, a 17-year-old professional *shogi* prodigy. *Shogi* is a two-player strategy game that's also known as Japanese chess.

Rei is orphaned when his family members are killed in a car accident. He's taken in by Masachika Kōda, his father's best friend and a fellow professional *shogi* player. Rei struggles with loneliness and has difficulty with his school and the pressures to succeed. As Rei grows, he learns to navigate interactions with others, enhancing his life as an individual and a shogi player.

OURAN HIGH SCHOOL HOST CLUB

Ouran High School Host Club follows the life of Haruhi Fujioka, a teenage girl who receives a scholarship that allows her to attend Ouran Academy — a fancy school with wealthy students. Haruhi finds herself working for the Ouran Host Club to pay for accidentally breaking an expensive vase. She is mistaken for a boy at first due to her appearance, which creates comic situations for her and the other characters.

SILVER SPOON

The slice-of-life anime series *Silver Spoon* takes a different approach. Protagonist Yuugo Hachiken enrolls in Ooezo Agricultural High School even though he's from the city and has no experience with the challenges of farm life. *Silver Spoon* features some comedic situations, but it's balanced with its realistic portrayal of the agricultural industry and more serious narrative themes of ethics and self-discovery.

SPORTS ANIME

Sports have a universal appeal due to the drama of competition, the strength and spirit of athletes, and camaraderie. However, sports anime is often about much more than just competitive action or showcasing athletics. It features important emotional aspects such as perseverance and dedication. This genre of anime also features interesting and meaningful relationships between characters, as well as other relatable themes for diverse fan groups.

SPORTS ANIME BLENDS ACTION AND EMOTION

Sports anime series combine action and emotion. This allows viewers to not only enjoy the excitement of the storylines but also to relate and connect with the characters.

Haikyuu!! is an anime series about Shoyo Hinata, a student in junior high who's inspired by Karasuno High School's volleyball team. After two years, Hinata convinces his friends to join the junior high school's volleyball team so that he can play in a tournament. When rival player Kageyama comes to

Karsuno High School, their combined skills help lead the team to a national competition.

Similarly, *Kuroko's Basketball* begins with the star players of a winning middle school basketball team. The five athletes become known as the "Generation of Miracles" as they each move on to different high schools to play basketball. A mysterious sixth member of the Generation of Miracles, Tetsuya Kuroko, joins the basketball team at Seirin High School and must take on his former middle school teammates to become number one. This sports anime series has themes of friendships, rivalry, and natural talent.

Lastly, *Free* is a popular example of a sports anime series that features swimming while focusing on a group of friends and their relationships. The storylines also involve themes such as dealing with injuries, feeling inadequate or anxious, and losing loved ones. Swimming serves as the catalyst for bringing the characters together as friends and creating tension in their relationships as they form a swim team and undergo personal challenges.

WHY SPORTS ANIME RESONATES WITH AUDIENCES

Sports anime combines well-developed characters with a careful balance between the drama of competition and real emotion. Even though sports connect the narratives in this genre, they are often secondary to the portrayal of characters and their struggles.

Sports anime series address a range of issues that affect individual characters and team dynamics. This can include challenges with identity, body image, anxiety, loneliness, and failure. These common emotions and experiences are incorporated into compelling plots involving various sports.

PSYCHOLOGICAL AND THRILLER ANIME

Psychological anime is one of the darker subcultures on the anime spectrum. The material tends to be thought provoking, morbid, and even disturbing. Like traditional psychological, thriller, and horror stories, anime in this subgenre feature complex stories with dark settings and morally ambiguous characters.

ANIME WITH COMPLEX NARRATIVES

Two of the most successful and popular psychological thriller anime are *Death Note* and *Paranoia Agent*. *Death Note*, an adaptation of the manga with the same title, was released in 2007 with 37 episodes. The plot is centered around an intelligent high school student who takes up a crusade to eliminate criminals from society.

The student, Light Yagami, discovers a notebook and realizes that people die in less than a minute when he writes their name inside. Understanding this power, Light begins killing those whom he feels must be brought to justice. The series explores themes such as corruption through power, justice, and morality.

Meanwhile, *Paranoia Agent* is a highly rated original creation from Satoshi Kon and is considered one of the most frightening anime series ever made. It premiered in 2004 with 13 episodes. The setting is Musashino City where citizens are terrified of "Lil' Slugger"—a boy who roams the streets on inline skates, wears a baseball cap, and beats victims with a golden baseball bat.

Two detectives, Keiichi Ikari and Mitsuhiro Maniwa, attempt to discover Lil' Slugger's identity and bring him to justice. However, the detectives are faced with red herrings and supernatural obstacles during their investigation. The series blurs the lines between perception and reality, individual and societal anxiety, and modern ways of coping with pain.

HOW THESE SHOWS EXPLORE HUMAN NATURE

As an art form, anime and its subgenres allow for the exploration of many admirable human qualities such as friendship and courage. However, psychological and thriller anime works offer a window into the darker side of human nature by exploring qualities like fear, death, isolation, and moral compromise.

Psychological and thriller anime reflect the tension between the individual and society, especially in terms of moral codes. As a subculture, this type of anime presents emotional narratives and characters facing moral dilemmas in which the lines between right and wrong are blurred.

In addition, the characters featured in psychological and thriller anime are often developed at a deeper level. The audience is able to witness their internal struggles and motivations. As a result, viewers can engage more actively with the content through interpretation and analysis. The artistic nature of this subculture also tends to be visually stunning and stylistic, adding another level of emotional connection to the story.

CHAPTER SIX: THE MUSIC OF ANIME

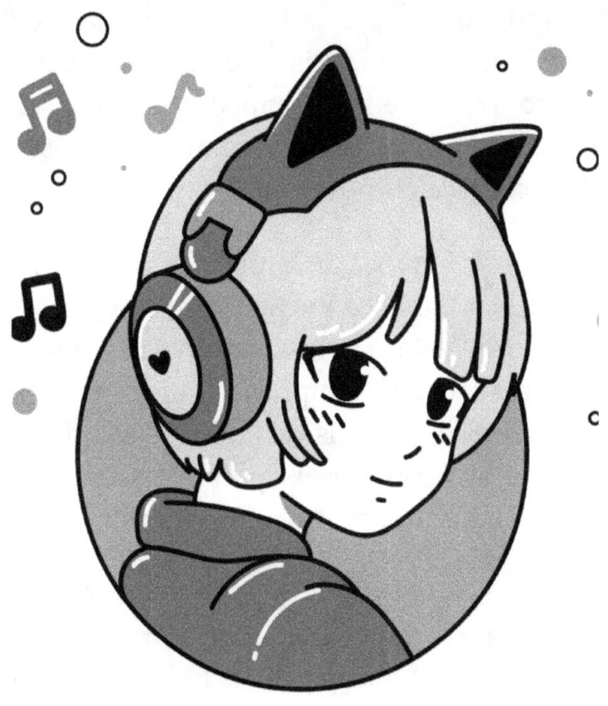

As with many visual art forms and media, music plays an integral part in the success and enjoyment of anime. Musical soundtracks add emotional depth to the characters' journeys and context for viewers to understand the story's narrative. In fact, anime music can reach iconic levels among fans that's equal to the series and characters themselves.

Music and art appreciation are prioritized in Japanese culture, which is one reason music and anime are so closely entwined. Japanese anime features diverse musical genres and compositions, including classical, hip-hop, jazz, and J-pop.

The purpose of music in anime is not to fill the background or enhance the action of the plot, as it's often used in Western animation. Instead, it's meant to contextualize and emphasize the emotions of anime characters. This is achieved through theme songs that play an important part in certain series as well as opening and closing themes that convey a specific premise.

Perhaps the most significant aspect of anime music is how it resonates with fans. As an art form, music is comparable to animation in that it can transcend language and geographical, cultural, and generational boundaries. It has a unique power to inspire and emotionally move people.

THE IMPORTANCE OF OPENING AND ENDING THEMES

Opening themes (OPs) and ending themes (EDs) are important elements of music in anime. An opening theme is designed to get the audience's attention and ultimately be associated with the continuity of the series. OPs may contain lyrics and feature Japanese and/or international musicians.

Ending themes are important in evoking a sense of reflection for viewers after an anime episode has concluded. They are typically less upbeat than OPs and evoke feelings of closure through emotional music and reflective lyrics.

OPENING AND ENDING THEMES SET THE TONE FOR ANIME

Opening and ending themes are prevalent in most audiovisual media. OPs set the mood for the overall series and individual episodes, while ending themes encourage viewers to absorb the events of each episode's story.

Anime series incorporate music beyond OPs and EDs in character themes and background scores.

These are additional instrumental compositions that help to evoke moods and emotions during different scenes. Certain characters may have repetitive motifs or musical themes that enhance their personalities and emotional arcs as well.

However, these compositions are intended to be subtle background music to support and further the narrative. OPs and EDs are distinct and consistent pieces that carry through and set the tone through multiple episodes.

ICONIC MUSICAL THEMES THROUGHOUT ANIME HISTORY

There are many OPs and EDs that are as iconic and memorable on their own. These opening and ending themes are integral to anime history.

Here are some examples of iconic OPs in anime history:

- "A Cruel Angel's Thesis" — *Neon Genesis Evangelion*
- "Tank!" — *Cowboy Bebop*
- "Cha-La Head-Cha-La" — *Dragon Ball Z*
- "Dream of Life" — *Bakuman*
- "Moonlight Densetsu" — *Sailor Moon*

Popular EDs in anime history include the following:

- "Dango Daikazoku" — *Clannad*
- "Ride on Shooting Star" — *FLCL*
- "See You Later" — *Attack on Titan*
- "Styx Helix" — *Re: Zero*
- "Nai Nai" — *Shadows House*

FAMOUS ANIME SOUNDTRACKS

Many legendary anime soundtracks have been composed by influential people such as Yoko Kanno, Joe Hisaishi, and Shiro Sagisu. These composers combine different musical elements to complement the mood of various anime films and series.

- Yoko Kanno is an extremely versatile composer who blends jazz, orchestral, rock, and blues influences. She is known for her musical contributions to series such as *Cowboy Bebop* and *The Vision of Escaflowne*.
- Joe Hisaishi has composed memorable film soundtracks for many Studio Ghibli works, including *My Neighbor Totoro*, *Spirited Away*, and *Princess Mononoke*. Hisaishi's classical and modern compositions enhance the beauty of the worlds portrayed in these anime films.

- Shiro Sagisu is known for his soundtrack music in *Neon Genesis Evangelion*. He blends orchestral and choral music to achieve emotional depth.

HOW SOUNDTRACKS ENHANCE THE EXPERIENCE

Movie and series soundtracks enhance the anime experience by providing an even deeper emotional connection to the story and characters. Although some viewers may only be aware of anime soundtracks as background music to the action being portrayed, even the most subtle musical compositions have an impact that sets a narrative's tone and mood.

For those who are interested in musical composition or just enjoy soundtracks overall, the experience of anime is heightened even further, as the music can be enjoyed as an extension of or even independently from the anime show. Many anime soundtracks are released as individual albums, some of which become collectibles. Several have even been performed in concert or at conventions.

Like fan art and fiction, some fans cover or even remix anime music for themselves and others to enjoy. In addition, soundtracks are often shared across the anime fandom and generate deep discussions within forums and other online communities. Listening to favorite songs can also help fans feel connected to their favorite anime when they're engaged in other tasks such as exercising or studying.

THE ROLE OF VOICE ACTORS

Seiyuu is the Japanese word for voice actors. The role of voice actors is to bring anime characters to life and narrate their stories. *Seiyuu* work with directors and the production crew of anime series and movies to coordinate their voice acting with the characters and animation.

Although it may appear simple on the surface, voice acting is a complex and challenging art. *Seiyuu* don't have the luxury of conveying emotions through their eyes, facial expressions, or body language. Instead, their voice becomes their sole instrument and acting tool.

In addition, voice acting is often a solitary pursuit. Unlike traditional actors who would play roles in scenes with other professionals, voice actors are usually in a sound booth with a headset and microphone. They generally record their own dialogue without hearing or seeing their colleagues.

THE IMPORTANCE OF VOICE ACTORS IN ANIME CULTURE

Seiyuu actors are extremely important in anime culture, as voice acting captures the emotions and personality of the characters being portrayed. These voice actors not only provide spoken narrative and dialogue in anime stories, but they also add nuances in terms of language and tone. This is particularly significant in terms of the Japanese language and preserving cultural as well as linguistic authenticity.

Seiyuu study the anime script to understand their characters' emotions, personality, and actions. From there, they develop a specific voice that matches these qualities and corresponds with the overall narrative. This is essential for viewers to connect with and understand each character's development.

Voice actors record their lines with the goals of conveying their character's words, maintaining consistency, and ensuring the timing fits with the lines of other characters. This can involve multiple takes with instructions from the director and required modifications to sync with computer animation.

NOTABLE *SEIYUU* AND THEIR ICONIC ROLES

There are many famous Japanese anime *seiyuu*, including Kenjirou Tsuda, Masako Nozawa, Megumi Hayashibara, Rie Kugimiya, and Mamoru Miyano.

- Kenjirou Tsuda is considered by many to be the most iconic *seiyuu*. His characters include Kento Nanami from *Jujutsu Kaisen*, Joker from *Fire Force*, Tatsu from *The Way of the Househusband,* and Kishibe from *Chainsaw Man.*

- Masako Nozawa is considered a pioneer of *seiyuu* and one of the most prolific Japanese voice actors for several decades. She voices the iconic Son Goku, as well as relatives Son Gohan and Son Goten, in the Dragon Ball franchise, in addition to many other characters.

- Megumi Hayashibara is another popular *seiyuu* who has been voicing characters since the 1990s. She is known for roles in *Cowboy Bebop, Slayers, Pokémon,* and more.

- Rie Kugimiya voices popular anime characters such as Alphonse Elric in the series *Fullmetal Alchemist,* Kagura in *Gintama,* and Happy in *Fairy Tail.*

- Mamoru Miyano is known for roles in *Death Note*, *Fullmetal Alchemist*, *Bungo Stray Dogs*, and *Durarara!!*.

Not all anime voice actors are in Japan. Yuri Lowenthal, Crispin Freeman, and Johnny Yong Bosch are three American anime voice acting stars.

- Yuri Lowenthal is well known for anime as well as other animated movies and series. He has provided voices for Yuuta Takemoto in *Honey and Clover*, Shinra Kishitani in *Durarara!!*, and Sasuke Uchicha in *Naruto*.
- Crispin Freeman is famous for his roles as Itachi Uchiha in *Naruto*, Kirei Kotomine, in *Fate/Zero*, and Alucard in *Hellsing*.
- Johnny Yong Bosch has done a variety of voice acting, including voicing Ichigo Kurosaki in *Bleach*, Vash the Stampede in *Trigun*, Nero, in *Devil May Cry*, and Lelouch Vi Britannia in *Code Geass*.

Not only are these *seiyuu* popular among and beloved by fans for their work in bringing iconic anime roles to life, but many have won prestigious voice acting awards for excellence in their craft.

MUSIC AND CONCERTS IN THE ANIME WORLD

Music expands and enhances the world of anime. Since music transcends language, its presence in the anime world is integral to conveying emotion in storytelling and inspiring emotional reactions in viewers.

Many full anime soundtracks, as well as individual OPs and EDs, are available on mainstream music platforms for a wide listening audience. Concerts featuring anime music also bring fans together to hear various performers and original compositions. Whether concerts comprise orchestral film soundtracks or opening and ending theme songs, the musical compositions are enjoyable by themselves without a need to have seen the visual anime content. This allows for greater inclusivity and diverse participation from music lovers in the world of anime.

CHAPTER SEVEN: ANIME MERCHANDISE AND COLLECTIBLES

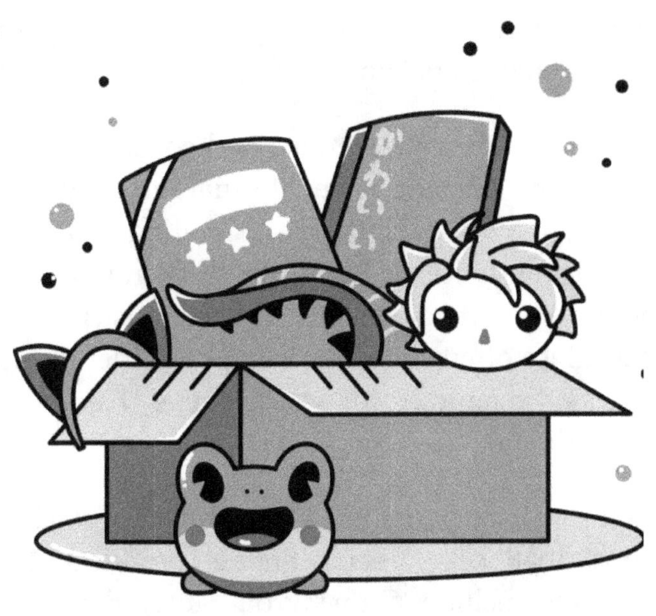

The merchandise and collectibles associated with anime are an important way for fans to indulge their specific passions and support the industry. Merchandise is also a way to connect with others and reflect loyalty to fan base communities. Anime merchandise and collectibles come in a variety of forms, such as figures, posters, accessories, plushies, and T-shirts. Certain items are also considered limited edition or rare. Some fans have even created their own merchandise that's inspired by their favorite characters, movies, and series.

It's important for anime fans and collectors to note that anime content is intellectual property that's protected by copyright law. Creating, selling, or purchasing unlicensed items is likely in violation of such laws and may incur financial risks. Official collectibles often feature some form of identification such as a manufacturer seal, number, bar code, or branded logo.

There are many online and in-person stores and shops that sell official anime products. Some examples include Crunchyroll Store, Box Lunch, Atsuko, and even Amazon. In addition, anime conventions often include merchandise vendors who are licensed and may sell limited-edition and traditional items.

THE WORLD OF ANIME FIGURES

There is an entire world of anime figures, and many are considered desirable and valuable to collectors. There are different types such as Nendoroid, Figma, scale, and resin figures. It's important for collectors to know the different types so that they can acquire items in alignment with their budget, space, and aesthetic preference.

- Nendoroid: compact
- Figma: detailed with articulated joints to allow for posing
- Scale: realistic details
- Resin: bright colors and intricate details

MERCHANDISE

Anime fans often seek limited-edition merchandise due to its rarity and value within the community. However, there's also a wide variety of popular anime merch that allows fans to showcase their interests without breaking their budgets. This includes items such as key chains, wearable accessories, stationery, and more.

WEARING YOUR FAVORITE ANIME

Like fans of sports teams, anime fans find it appealing to wear clothing and accessories that represent their favorite series, movies, and characters. This not only allows anime enthusiasts to showcase their interests and passions to others, but it offers a sense of belonging and recognition for those who appreciate the art form.

Wearing your favorite anime is a form of self-expression. Whether you take part in full cosplay or just like the look of an item with anime graphics, you can feel proud wearing what brings you joy. Ultimately, the appeal of wearing anime apparel should be the freedom to be your authentic self and show your appreciation for what you find meaningful.

HOW TO WATCH ANIME

Streaming services have not only allowed more fans to access and enjoy anime movies and series, but they also offer a growing catalog of content for diverse audiences across the globe. Although viewers can watch their favorite anime on streaming services, these platforms don't allow fans to own the actual content. Monthly subscription prices can also add up, and there's no guarantee that a show will continue to be available.

DVDs can be beneficial for anime lovers who want to own copies of their favorites. They don't require funds beyond the initial purchase and can be viewed independently of streaming services and the internet. However, anime DVDs also have their downsides. They require a DVD player and storage, making them far less portable and all but inaccessible on the go. In addition, physical DVDs are becoming more difficult to obtain, especially as new series and movies are released solely on streaming platforms.

THE BEST PLATFORMS FOR STREAMING ANIME

Thankfully, there are many platform options available for fans to watch anime legally. Mainstream services such as Netflix, Hulu, Max, and Prime Video have all expanded their streaming content to include many anime movies and series. Crunchyroll, Tubi, Hidive, and RetroCrush are available as well. Of course, these platforms vary in terms of cost, advertisements, and the availability of anime content.

Unfortunately, there are also websites that engage in piracy and distribute illegal anime content. Users who support these sites can actually face criminal charges. The Content Overseas Distribution Association (CODA) is Japan's anti-piracy organization, and they work closely with other groups to close anime piracy sites. CODA has had success in shutting down illegal sites as well as negotiating with site operators to hand over access.

It's essential to keep in mind that media piracy is a serious issue worldwide. While it can seem like a relatively harmless offense, illegally streaming anime affects the overall industry in many ways. This includes loss of intellectual property, copyright violations, and undermining the creative and technical work that goes into making anime. With the numerous options available to safely and legally stream anime of all types, there is really no excuse for those who intentionally try to cheat the system.

THE HISTORY AND FUTURE OF PHYSICAL MEDIA

The future of physical media is a hot topic across the entertainment industry. With the proliferation of digital platforms, consumers no longer have to depend on physical media. Access to content and programming is available at an unprecedented level for those with online streaming services, offering a nearly overwhelming number of choices for instant entertainment.

This trend away from physical media is a mixed blessing for anime fans whose content options have expanded with streaming services but who are also at risk of losing access to their favorites. Devoted anime fans and collectors, therefore, may feel the need to invest in physical media.

CHAPTER EIGHT: UNDERSTANDING ANIME THEMES AND STORYTELLING

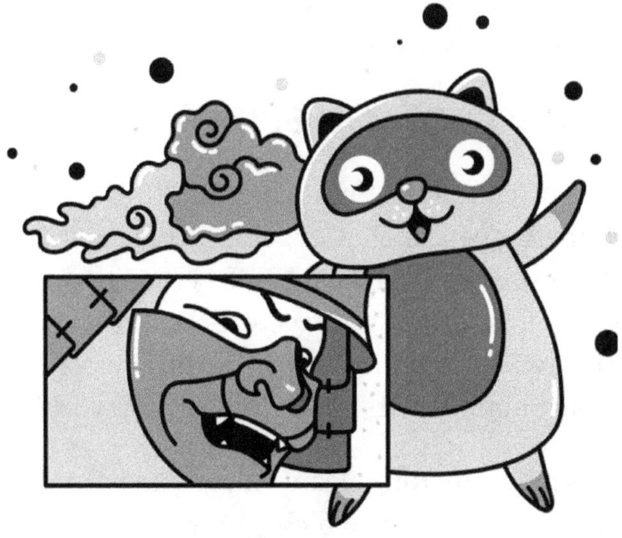

COMMON THEMES IN ANIME

Japanese anime stands apart from Western animation not only in art style but in the themes creators choose to weave into their stories. Even anime targeting younger audiences is often filled with emotionally resonant and philosophically rich subtext. To fully understand this, it's important to keep in mind that Japanese culture heavily influences the art form.

PHILOSOPHY AND SPIRITUALITY

Anime often reflects Shinto and Buddhist ideas such as impermanence, duality, reincarnation, harmony with nature, and the beauty of everyday moments. For example, *Princess Mononoke*'s backdrop portrays nature with a whimsical, spiritual essence that mirrors Shinto beliefs about the natural world.

Western animators lean more toward Judeo-Christian narratives, which glorify themes such as good versus evil and redemption arcs. Anime's themes are less binary and often explore gray areas, cycles, and personal transformation.

AMBIGUITY AND EMOTIONAL COMPLEXITY

Anime embraces nuance and ambiguity, especially when it comes to characters and story endings. It's common for heroes to be morally flawed and for villains to invoke sympathy. Many stories have endings that are unresolved or slightly "messy." Western animation, especially with its general lean toward younger audiences, often favors clear moral binaries and clean resolutions.

COMING OF AGE WITH CONSEQUENCES

Although it's common for most cultures to dive into coming-of-age stories, anime often digs deeper into the burden of responsibility and generational trauma. Where there are a few Western animations that deal with these topics (*Rick and Morty* is one), it's rare to see these themes appear in cartoons made for a younger demographic.

In anime, though, these themes are common even for young audiences. In Japanese anime, coming-of-age characters don't just grow up—they break down, rebuild, and question the world around them.

SOCIETY VS. THE INDIVIDUAL

Japanese culture often emphasizes collectivism, social roles, and harmony, but anime characters often rebel against those expectations. It's common for characters to have a push and pull between duty and desire as well as personal ambition versus community service. Western animations often glorify individualism, whereas anime critiques both paths.

THE ROLE OF JAPANESE FOLKLORE IN ANIME

Japanese folklore is what gives anime its extra touch of magic and depth. It's present in character development, backdrops, world-building, and plot. Japanese folklore is often adapted and merged with modern positions to blend cultural memory with present-day issues.

MONSTERS, DEMONS, AND SPIRITS

Below is a short list of common creatures that appear in anime. When watching anime, if you're confused about a specific character or reference, chances are that it's linked to Japanese mythology or folklore. It's a good idea to get used to looking up new terms throughout your anime journey.

- *Yōkai* are a class of supernatural beings that includes monsters, spirits, and demons. These creatures are personifications of the unexplainable, ranging from unidentifiable noises to strange illnesses. They're not necessarily "ghosts" or even "evil" like in Western stories. Some are cute and helpful. Others are vengeful and dangerous. It's common to see them presented as morally gray and blurring the lines between good and evil.
- *Kami* are divine spirits or forces of nature, according to Shinto beliefs. However, they are not gods. They're more likely to appear as natural elements; geographic features like rivers; or personifications of ancestors, animals, or ideas.
- A *kitsune* is a magical fox spirit known for its intelligence, shape-shifting capabilities, and extraordinarily long life. In Shinto traditions, they are the messengers of the rice god Inari. *Kitsune* can take human form, often appearing as beautiful women, and are known to appear as both mischievous tricksters and revered protectors.

- *Tengu* are supernatural beings often associated with mountains and forests. They are known for being disruptive but have more recently been viewed as guardian spirits. They're often depicted with red faces, long noses, and bird-like wings or beaks. *Tengu* are warriors and will commonly appear in anime as teachers of various martial arts or a being charged with punishing those who disrespect nature or the spiritual world.

- *Oni* are ogre-like demons known for their strength, wild appearance, and tendency toward chaos. They are usually depicted with red or blue skin, horns, and sharp teeth. They torment sinners in the afterlife or wreak havoc in the mortal realm. In modern anime, it's not uncommon to see *oni* transformed into antiheroes rather than depicting them as static "bad" characters.

- *Tsukumogami* are objects that come to life after 100 years. Although they are usually mischievous, they aren't always malevolent.

JAPANESE LEGENDS

Again, there are far too many myths and legends to create a comprehensive list in this book. With that said, below are some common stories that appear in anime. Reading these stories will help you have a deeper understanding of plots and references within anime.

- "The Tale of the Bamboo Cutter" is one of Japan's oldest stories. It's about a princess found inside a bamboo stalk.
- "The Legend of Momotaro" is about a boy born from a peach who goes on a quest with a dog, a monkey, and a pheasant to fight *oni*.
- Yamata no Orochi is an eight-headed, eight-tailed serpent. In stories, the storm god Susano defeats the serpent and rescues the maiden Kushinada.
- "Amaterasu and the Cave" is about the sun goddess Amaterasu, who hides in a cave and plunges the world into darkness. Other gods lure her out with a mirror and a dance.
- The story of Urashima Tarō is about a fisherman who saves a turtle and is taken to an undersea palace. When he returns, centuries have passed.
- "The Crab and the Monkey" is a folktale about a monkey who kills a crab but is ultimately punished by the crab's children.

- According to legend, *Jorogumo* is a spider who can shapeshift into a beautiful woman to seduce and eat men.

SYMBOLISM AND HIDDEN MEANINGS IN ANIME

Learning common symbols present in anime will help enrich your experience. Like many art forms, anime uses symbols to draw deeper connections between the landscape and the internal state of the characters.

- Cherry blossoms often represent impermanence, fleeting beauty, new beginnings, or loss. They reflect the Buddhist concept of *mono no aware* — an awareness of life's transience.
- Foxes appear as a symbol for trickery and as divine messengers. They represent the dualistic nature of the world, as they are both wise and benevolent or mischievous and deceptive.
- Masks are used to represent hidden identities, transformation, spiritual protection, or dehumanization. They are often worn by samurai, yokai, cultists, or festivalgoers.

increases the likelihood that anime and streaming services will be intertwined in numerous ways going forward.

STREAMING PLATFORMS HAVE CHANGED THE ANIME INDUSTRY

Both Crunchyroll and Netflix, among other streaming services, have transformed the anime industry through their streaming platforms. The Crunchyroll platform, formerly known as Funimation, features anime and East Asian media. Its library includes anime series, movies, and original productions. Crunchyroll also offers a store with anime merchandise, and campaigns such as Crunchyroll Originals provide funding to produce exclusive anime series.

Crunchyroll pioneered convenient streaming access for anime content and reduced fan dependence on acquiring DVDs or making illegal downloads. In addition, the platform's catalog is extensive, including popular as well as niche anime. It offers versions that are subbed and dubbed in various languages for fans around the world. Crunchyroll has also implemented simulcasting, which has decreased piracy due to new episodes being legally released on the platform shortly after their Japanese air dates.

Like Crunchyroll, Netflix's growing library of anime content has brought significant revenue to the anime industry. Netflix has also influenced the industry by making anime content accessible to mainstream viewers, many of whom would otherwise never have been exposed to Japanese animation.

THE FUTURE OF STREAMING AND ANIME DISTRIBUTION

Although most fans and creators would agree that streaming has had an immensely positive effect on anime by increasing both its demand and supply, there may be legitimate concerns regarding the future of streaming and anime distribution.

For example, competition among streaming services has intensified, leading to greater investments in content but also dividing the availability of shows across more platforms. This can end up limiting access to certain series and movies for fans who can't afford to pay for multiple services to watch all their favorites. Cost could create an uptick in piracy and other unethical viewing behavior.

There is also a concern among some fans and industry participants that global streaming services such as Netflix may adapt or censor anime content to appeal to a wider mainstream audience. This could include making certain shows more family friendly or appropriate for younger audiences.

Making changes could potentially alter and compromise the artistic style and storytelling of certain anime movies and series. It would also limit the creativity of the original anime if platforms alter content to suit the tastes and sensibilities of Western viewers.

THE ROLE OF VIRTUAL REALITY AND AUGMENTED REALITY

Virtual reality (VR) and augmented reality (AR) are playing increasingly larger roles in how fans experience and enjoy entertainment. Virtual reality is more immersive than watching a traditional show. For example, in VR, you wear a special headset that's designed to block out the real world. In VR video games, the player is surrounded by the game world.

Augmented reality doesn't replace your environment but rather adds to or enhances your perception of it. This is accomplished through digital information overlays that complement your real surroundings. AR is accessed through devices such as smart glasses or a smartphone. For example, many people play *Pokémon Go* and follow a digital map on smart devices to locate Pokémon while walking around in the real world.

Both VR and AR are influential in how people are consuming and taking part in entertainment, and anime is no exception for this trend. Of course, there are devices and equipment required to participate in each experience, and VR technology can be quite expensive. In addition, some people are wary of long-term effects such as eye strain and fatigue that are potentially caused by overuse of VR and digital screens.

Interestingly, there are anime shows that address the blurring boundaries between virtual and actual realities. For example, *Sword Art Online* involves protagonists participating in virtual gaming worlds and a simulated civilization. This offers what some may consider a "meta" perspective of the increasingly influential roles played by VR and AR in anime and other experiences.

THE FUTURE OF CGI IN ANIME

CGI can help artists and animators design worlds, characters, scenes, and special effects. It may surprise some fans to learn that computers have been involved in anime productions since the 1980s. Animators were able to incorporate digital effects into their hand-drawn visuals with early CGI software. This allowed them to bring complex models and action to life that otherwise would have been impossible with traditional illustrations.

THE INCREASING USE OF CGI IN ANIME

CGI can be a helpful tool in creating or enhancing anime series and films, which is why its use and popularity is on the rise. In addition, advancements in graphics software and CGI capabilities have made it almost indispensable in the overall creation and production of animation.

CGI also offers a level of image control, reproduction, and manipulation that can't be replicated with hand-drawn or other animation techniques. This enhances the consistency and continuity of animation by presenting a unified aesthetic.

HOW TECHNOLOGY IS CHANGING THE VISUAL STYLE OF ANIME

Of course, the introduction of technology and digital animation has changed the visual style of anime to some degree. The opposition to stylistic changes in anime is understandable for many fans who feel it's contrary to the root of anime art.

Some anime productions are fully embracing computer-generated animation and letting go of the traditional 2-D style in favor of 3-DCG anime. This style is a combination of traditional 2-D animation with 3D models and movement. The resulting visual style can be similar to a video game, which many anime fans don't appreciate, especially in relation to established anime franchises.

This technology may change the visual style of anime, but many view the trade-offs as faster and more cost-effective production. Lower production costs lead to greater opportunities for up-and-coming animators who would rather work with software than 2-D drawings.

Whether there will be a full shift from traditional anime techniques to CGI will depend on decisions at the studio executive level and the support or resistance of anime fans. It's likely that a combination of tools and techniques will be used in the years to come.

NEW TRENDS IN ANIME STORYTELLING

As the cultural impact of anime expands across the globe, new trends are taking place in anime storytelling. These evolutions reflect narratives that are personally meaningful to creators, along with wider and more diverse approaches to reach larger audiences.

Anime genres continue to develop their focus on storytelling, many of which address complex themes and societal issues. Another positive trend is increased inclusivity and representation, ranging from neurodivergent stories to portrayals of LGBTQ+ relationships.

Psychological stories are more common than ever in anime, with characters who demonstrate more realistic behaviors and motivations. Such characters facilitate meaningful story arcs, reflecting flaws and struggles that are relatable to viewers.

THE RISE OF EXPERIMENTAL AND AVANT-GARDE ANIME

Like most forms of art, anime has experienced a rise in experimental and avant-garde content and productions. This has led to deeper themes and emotional experiences for viewers, many of which may be too complex to address in other forms of entertainment outside of anime. Such groundbreaking anime shows have also incorporated various social issues in unique ways, offering audiences thought-provoking storylines and intricate character development.

In addition, technology and other advancements in animation have made complex productions possible to allow for surreal art and experimental worlds. Virtual reality and integration with other media also add to the rise in cutting-edge anime shows and unique, immersive experiences for viewers to interact with anime content. This sets a foundation for anime to embrace new styles and material, as well as for artists to expand their vision and narrative scope.

PUSHING THE BOUNDARIES OF TRADITIONAL ANIME NARRATIVES

There are many shows being created and released that push the boundaries of anime narratives. Some of these series, such as *Demon Slayer* and *Violet Evergarden*, tackle issues such as emotional trauma and self-expression in inventive ways. Movies such as *Your Name* also push traditional genre boundaries — in this case, in the romance genre — by experimenting with narrative structure and imagery.

Of course, not all anime genres or new series are being developed to push traditional storytelling boundaries. However, the expansion of anime narratives, characters, and themes reflects the dynamic creativity inspired by this art form. As a result, anime will continue to generate new, meaningful narratives that appeal to a variety of viewers with open minds.

CHAPTER TEN:
BECOMING A
DEDICATED ANIME FAN

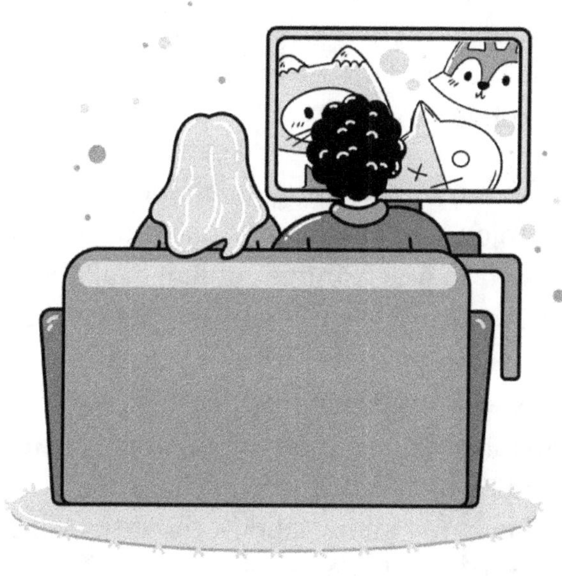

When it comes to anime content, there seems to be something for everyone—no matter your age, career, lifestyle, or geographic location. This not only makes it easy to become a fan of anime but also to continue as one in the long term.

Anime series and movies can be both entertaining and emotionally resonant no matter what stage of life you're in. As a dedicated fan, you may learn new things about yourself as you try different genres and shows or possibly revisit your favorites. You may also expand your love of anime by learning more about Japanese art or traveling to a new place to attend a convention.

Part of the fun of becoming an anime fan is the way you can enjoy series or movies on your own or with others. With so much anime content available, many fans decide to track and rate the series that they watch. This can be done through journaling, making a spreadsheet, or posting updates on social media platforms such as Instagram or X. Anime forums and communities like Reddit are additional options for anime fans to share their thoughts and get recommendations from others.

You may build friendships across the globe and even venture into collecting merchandise. You may try cosplay or create fan art or fiction. No matter how active you wish to be within the anime fandom, there are many ways to participate and demonstrate your dedication as a fan.

STAYING UP TO DATE WITH NEW ANIME RELEASES

Although many anime fans are quite loyal to the series they love, it's also a good idea to stay current on new anime releases. Word of mouth is powerful within the anime fandom, whether you get updates from reviewers, online community discussions, or reputable sites devoted to anime content.

Keeping up with the volume of anime available may seem daunting, but new series and movies of various genres are always being created and released to meet demand. Knowing how to sift through fan recommendations and reviews to find what's most appealing to you can also feel overwhelming at times. To avoid such overload, here are some basic strategies:

- If you prefer a certain genre of anime, try different series in the same category.
- If you're interested in other genres, it's wise to read synopses and a few well-crafted reviews to get a sense of whether certain new series will appeal to your taste.

- If you belong to online anime communities or forums, ask for suggestions and recommendations from fellow fans.

Ultimately, it's best to find a balance between trying new releases and enjoying familiar shows. There's so much anime to choose from, and so many opinions within the fandom, that focusing on shows that are meaningful to you should be a priority. You can always research, branch out, and give new anime content a try when you're ready.

THE BEST SOURCES FOR NEWS AND UPCOMING ANIME SERIES

There are many beneficial sources for news on upcoming anime series, including several anime websites and blogs that feature preview lists. In addition, social media groups are a great resource for anime news. Most participants in online anime communities like Reddit or fan forums hold discussions about upcoming series and share watch lists.

Apps such as Simkl or ManGo provide notifications regarding new episodes and allow users to track anime series, TV shows, and movies. It's likely that your streaming service(s) will also provide updates when new series are available or when a new season of your favorite anime is expected to be released.

Anime News Network is considered a comprehensive and trusted source for upcoming anime series and nearly everything else related to anime news. The site features an encyclopedia of content, previews of new shows, professional and fan reviews, and a weekly newsletter. Users can register for free, contribute to the site's encyclopedia, and build personal lists of favorite series and movies.

KEEPING TRACK OF SEASONAL ANIME

Seasonal anime series usually air in three-month windows that correspond to seasons. This would include January to March (winter), April to June (spring), July to September (summer), and October to December (fall). In general, shows that air during the same season start at the same time and continue for 12 weeks, allowing a one-week break between seasons. Most anime seasons are made up of 12, 13, 24, or 26 episodes.

In the context of anime, a *cours* indicates the length of a television series. For example, a series of one season with 13 weekly episodes is considered one cours long, while a series of two seasons with 26 episodes would be considered two cours. In the case of 12- and 24-episode seasons, shows typically air across 12 weeks with 24-episode seasons divided between two cours of 12 episodes.

The number of episodes in a cours may vary, but it usually ranges between 11 and 14, with 13 episodes being the most common. Cours sometimes air in back-to-back seasons, with 13- or 26-episode seasons taking place a week early or continuing a week late.

Although it may seem complicated for new anime fans, there are ways to keep track of seasonal anime. Many fans use an online database such as MyAnimeList to sort upcoming anime series by season. These platforms also offer features such as a watch list to add shows you plan to watch or keep track of those you are watching, episode tracking, so you can update your progress for each show, and community reviews and recommendations.

There are also apps such as AniList and Kitsu. When you create an account, you can track what you've watched, give feedback, and interact with other users to keep up with seasonal anime and learn about new series.

SUPPORTING THE ANIME INDUSTRY

There are many ways that fans can support the anime industry. Of course, consuming anime content through legal methods and avoiding copyright infringement by purchasing licensed merchandise is fundamental to supporting the people involved in the anime industry.

Another example of being a supportive fan is gaining a better understanding of Japanese culture through anime. This not only creates a deeper connection with anime stories but also allows for a greater appreciation of the cultural roots that form the foundation of anime works.

Fans can also support the anime industry by being open to diverse genres, subcultures, and perspectives offered by the wide range of anime styles. This open-mindedness should also extend to the greater anime fandom community by respecting the passion that others may have for different characters and shows.

ETHICALLY SUPPORTING THE ANIME INDUSTRY

Ethical support of creators and their content is fundamental to art as a whole. When fans support the anime industry in an ethical manner, they're ensuring that artists and their intellectual property are valued and protected. This also benefits all the people who participate in bringing anime to life, from directors to voice actors, and every other role in the creation and production processes.

Another aspect of being an ethical anime fan is to be respectful and responsible when engaging with the anime community. Avoid any potentially harmful content and any toxic behavior or negative discourse in community forums.

Ethical fans should avoid exploitative content and should report online sites that promote any form of bullying or prejudice. Discussions among fans are healthy when they're constructive and respectful of diverse viewpoints. This doesn't mean you can't express an opinion about an anime production. However, critiques should never result in harassing or personally disparaging others.

ANIME COLLECTING TIPS FOR BEGINNERS

If you're interested in becoming an anime collector, there are several tips that can help you get started. The first step should be to determine why you want to build a collection and what items would be meaningful to you. For example, you may wish to collect pieces related to your favorite anime series for sentimental value or start a collection of figures from different series to reflect your diverse tastes.

There are multiple anime sites that new collectors can consult to get advice on how to start an anime collection. However, it's important to give thought to what you personally enjoy rather than trying to match another person's collection or follow a short-term trend.

Here are some helpful questions that beginners can ask themselves before collecting anime:

- Is the item affordable?
- Do I have space for it?
- Is the item meaningful to me or an impulse purchase?
- Does the item fit with my overall goal for my collection?
- Will I still appreciate this item in the future?

Above all, keep in mind that your primary reason for collecting anime is self-fulfillment and to enrich your hobby. Like any beginner, you can always start small and expand your vision as you go. Be aware that if you intend to collect rare or valuable anime-related items to make piles of money, you may wind up being disappointed.

STARTING YOUR ANIME COLLECTION

Anime offers many choices when it comes to collecting. Fans often build collections of anime figures, DVDs, and related merchandise. You may decide to focus your attention on collecting various items related to a specific anime or you may choose to collect a specific type of item such as posters. No matter what you decide, starting an anime collection can be a rewarding long-term hobby.

Since starting an anime collection can be expensive, keep your budget and spending limits in mind. Do your research to be sure you're buying items that are legitimate and meaningful to you.

Prices and the quality of merchandise can vary, so making informed and careful decisions will provide a good foundation for starting your anime collection. Finding a reliable, reputable anime seller or store will ensure that you're only purchasing genuine merchandise. In addition, shopping from trusted sellers will guarantee that the descriptions of items are accurate so that you'll know exactly what to expect.

PRESERVING AND DISPLAYING YOUR COLLECTION

As a rule, collectors view their items and pieces as investments. Anime fans are no exception. Therefore, it's helpful to learn some tips to preserve and display your collection so that you can enjoy your items, prevent deterioration, and protect their sentimental and potential monetary value.

Many anime fans and collectors have online pictures and videos of their displays as well as suggestions for keeping collector items in excellent condition. Most anime collectors wish to display their items in some way as a demonstration of their interests to others or as a means of taking pride in the collection they've worked to build.

It may be difficult for some who see your displayed collection to fully appreciate its importance or what it means to you, but that shouldn't discourage you from sharing your passion. Depending on what makes up your collection, you can group like or similar items. Another strategy is to arrange items together that are related to the same anime series or movie.

No matter how you decide to display your anime collection, formally or informally, the priority should be the personal joy you derive from it. Preserving your anime collection is also important, whether you intend to pass items on to someone in the future or perhaps sell them for their monetary value. Therefore, it's important to keep your collection in good, clean condition—free from dust, direct sunlight, and other harmful elements.

Some collectors choose to place their items in out-of-reach places on sturdy shelves or behind cabinet doors. Others may decide to preserve some or all of their collection in the original boxes. It's wise to find a balance between keeping your items perfectly preserved and allowing yourself to put them on display for your own personal enjoyment.

BUILDING ON YOUR ANIME KNOWLEDGE

Although watching your favorite series and movies is a wonderful experience, anime fans can expand their knowledge and enjoyment beyond what's available on the screen. Whether you decide to pursue further information about a particular character or show, there's a wide array of resources from which to learn more. This pursuit can also lead you to connect with other fans who share your interests and expand your understanding of anime as a whole.

If you have a favorite anime series or movie and would like to know the source material, you can research whether it's based on manga, light novel, or even Japanese folklore. This would allow you to expand your knowledge through reading the original story. In addition, you may decide to research the people involved in creating the anime you love to see what other projects they've participated in and learn more about the industry itself.

Fellow fans can also be knowledgeable sources through online blogs, discussions, and posts that offer different interpretations. You can also expand beyond online interactions by attending conventions. You may be inspired to try cosplay, build a collection of anime merchandise, or even learn about and create your own fan art.

EXPLORING ANIME ART BOOKS, LIGHT NOVELS, AND MANGA ADAPTATIONS

Exploring anime art books, light novels, and manga is a rewarding way to expand your anime knowledge and experience. When you explore anime in book form, it allows you to interact with the material in an entirely differently context.

For example, you can take the time to study illustrations and appreciate the art in greater detail rather than seeing the animation through quick actions on a screen. Reading the light novels or manga that inspired your favorite anime works is another way to explore the story in depth and consider the reasons behind any changes made from page to screen.

Japanese light novels are primarily directed toward young adults, but many also have an adult readership. These novels are typically shorter than traditional novels and often feature illustrations similar to manga.

In general, when manga books become popular, they are made into books — though chapters may continue to be featured in magazines. Light novels and manga have some common features such as including both color and black-and-white illustrations. When translated, however, most manga works retain their traditional Japanese reading format from right to left, whereas light novels are usually the opposite.

In most instances, a successful light novel may be adapted into a manga version, which may then be adapted into an anime series or movie. Occasionally, an extremely popular anime is adapted into a light novel or manga.

Another option is to read anime art books. These books are collections of new or rare art from an anime series or movie that's specially selected and meant to be displayed. Fans often showcase these as coffee table books or as part of a collection.

DEEPENING YOUR UNDERSTANDING

Thankfully, there are several ways to deepen your understanding of the anime you love. Most of the time when we first consume audiovisual art, we're focused on understanding the story and making sense of the plot. Without this initial step, it would be difficult to relate to the characters, events, setting, and other narrative elements. From there, however, fans can interact with the anime they love on multiple levels by focusing on and appreciating specific details.

For example, you might decide to rewatch your favorite series with an awareness of how you respond to each character. Perhaps some are more relatable or less likable on the surface than others, but your feelings may change as you pay closer attention to their behaviors and develop greater empathy for their complexities.

This can add new meaning and create a deeper understanding of the anime overall. Other potential details to notice might be the setting in which the story takes place and how that affects the overall artistic aesthetic of the anime.

Developing interpretation skills is also key to gaining a deeper understanding of anime. Fans may find that the more they watch and interact with their favorite anime, the more they recognize symbols and multiple meanings in the stories that create a larger context.

You might consider the cultural implications of *isekai* anime and why those particular stories resonate with people's emotions and experiences in today's society. In addition, the more you watch anime series and movies, the more likely you might be to absorb certain words and phrases in Japanese. This can not only build your understanding of anime but also allow you a greater connection to Japanese language and culture.

LIFELONG FANDOM

Unlike many interests and hobbies, anime can be a lifelong journey for fans. There's no age at which people are meant to outgrow anime, and there is such diversity in content and genres that fans can always find new material.

In addition, being a lifelong fan of anime can lead to other rewarding pursuits and knowledge. This includes a better understanding of Japanese language and culture, potential interest in manga and other reading material, and new passions for music.

There's also an opportunity along your anime journey to connect with new generations. Many individuals who discovered series such as *Pokémon, Yu-Gi-Oh!, Digimon,* and *Dragon Ball Z* just a couple of decades ago are now parents, aunts, and uncles who are able to share their anime love with younger kids. Meanwhile, the kids in your family may be fans of anime series or movies that are new to you.

Whether anime encourages you to engage with others or you simply value it as a source of individual entertainment, you can be assured that there are stories and characters to enjoy as long as you wish throughout all stages of life.

STAYING CONNECTED TO THE ANIME COMMUNITY

There are many ways for fans to stay connected to the anime community, such as joining and taking part in online fandoms and social media groups, attending conventions, or even starting a personal collection of anime merchandise.

Another way to maintain a connection to the anime community is to follow bloggers with expertise in anime series or fellow fans who create their own anime art. This can lead to discovering new shows or even developing an appreciation for experimental anime material.

Anime fans may also find connections among local groups such as manga book clubs or community art and animation classes. Some colleges and universities even offer courses in anime studies that offer numerous insights into the anime industry, its cultural traditions, and its unique impact on society.

Learning Japanese is another way to stay connected to the anime community. It presents a rewarding challenge, not only linguistically but also as a means of being able to enjoy anime in its native language. No matter where your anime journey takes you, there are several paths to maintaining connections within this lifelong fandom.

CONCLUSION

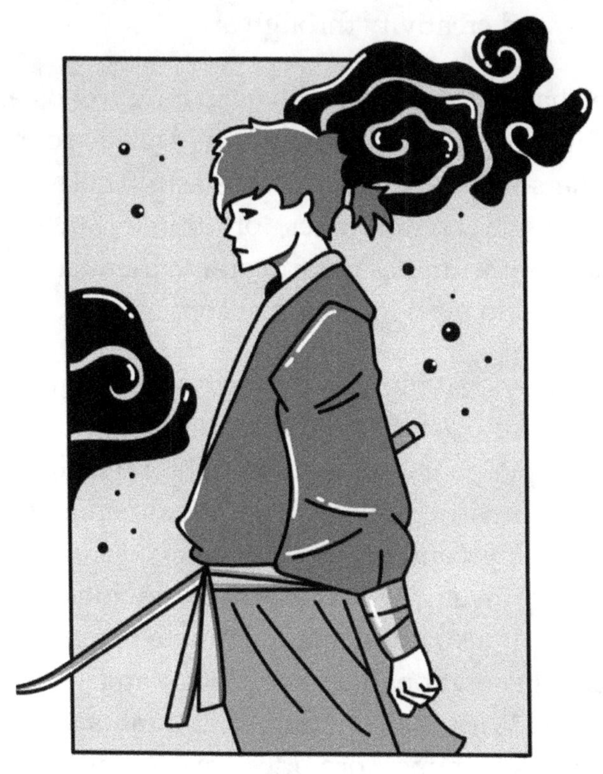

Anime is so much more than a form of entertainment made up of Japanese animated series or movies. Whether it's adapted from manga or an original creation, anime has become a dynamic cultural phenomenon in Japan and across the globe through its art and storytelling. It has impacted not just the animation industry but also the exchange of ideas, passions, and creativity through art.

Anime characters and narratives inspire trends and allow fans to express themselves, as well as connect with others who share their enthusiasm. This has led to worldwide communities of anime fans and provided opportunities to form online friendships or the potential to meet in person at conventions.

In many ways, anime reflects the power of art and the resonance of stories. Anime series and movies span multiple genres and subjects by appealing to universal human emotions. The artistic animation, detailed settings, and portrayal of beloved characters is inspiring in terms of creativity and innovative technology. It also reveals that animated stories can transcend generational, geographical, and cultural boundaries. With a global audience of all ages and backgrounds, anime provides a platform and foundation for people to share their experiences, appreciation, imagination, and understanding.

The anime fan community is also unique in its engagement with creators and fellow enthusiasts. From fan art to online platforms to large conventions, there's a worldwide network of shared interests and cultural exchanges among anime fans that continues to grow. As a result, anime is sure to endure, expand beyond Japanese animation, and remain relevant for generations to come.